California
Fire
&
Water

A Climate Crisis Anthology

California

Fire

&

Water

A Climate Crisis Anthology

edited by Molly Fisk

& Lisa Alvarez, Kirsten Casey, Chris Olander, Julie Valin

Foreword by SA Smythe

Printed in the United States of America
ISBN: 978-1-7329332-2-4

Published by Story Street Press
Nevada City, CA
e-mail: molly@mollyfisk.com
www.mollyfisk.com

Cover design: Maxima Kahn
Cover photo: "Courtney Fire, 2014," by Darvin Atkeson, Yosemite Landscapes
Interior design & typesetting: Julie Valin, Self to Shelf Publishing Svcs.
Font: Sabon, old-style serif typeface designed by German-born typographer
    and designer Jan Tschichold in the mid-1960s
Author photo: Aeron Miller Photography

Produced for on-demand distribution by Ingram/Lightning Source for Story Street Press.

Sales of this book contribute to the printing of copies for donation to California public, school, and prison libraries.

This book is dedicated to First Responders everywhere.

Sorry, it's
ash, sorry it's smoke all the way down.

Brenda Hillman

I want you to act as if the house is on fire,
because it is.

Greta Thunberg
Davos, Switzerland
January, 2019

CONTENTS

Foreword — SA Smythe

ii

Preface — Molly Fisk

iv

Poems

Foreword

When Molly first approached me to write the foreword for this anthology, I was sitting on my patio in Long Beach, CA, surrounded by annuals and succulents that wilted and sagged under the foggy frost of another unseasonably cold December morning. I remember thinking how much colder it was than last year, which was even colder than the year before that. Then I opened up the newspaper to read that New South Wales (Australia)'s government had declared a state of emergency due to the record-breaking temperatures and prolonged drought exacerbating an already out of control bushfire season. Not long after, a swarm of almost a dozen earthquakes tore through Puerto Rico; the island has yet to fully recover from Hurricane Maria in 2017. Puerto Ricans on their island and off are continuing to piece their lives back together despite disasters both natural and human-led. We are living in extreme times, to say the least. It's not just the weather—an ever-increasing majority of the earth's inhabitants are toiling away under political and meteorological conditions *in extremis* from Fiji to Flint.

For the Anglophone writer, Latin can be a helpful dead language used to convey the gravity of the matter, when English and all its vernaculars *simply won't do*. The Latin term *in extremis* means "in a dangerous or difficult situation that needs urgent attention," or "a period of a grave or fatal illness or injury." Everything about California's climate points to a life *in extremis*: each year, the temperatures clock in at record highs and record lows. The desert of Joshua Tree is coated with feet of snow while otherwise lush lands go brown and barren from drought, extending natural wildfire season to devastating effect as thousands flee subsequent mud-slides and floods, and the earth trembles beneath our feet with increasing frequency and intensity, rending apart the grounds beneath us. While politicians wring their hands and try to lay blame at one another's feet, the turmoil on these sacred lands is mirrored and magnified the world over.

How then, do we make sense of and fend off the fires *this* time? As is often the case with crisis, the one we're experiencing in the state, across the nation, and around the globe is manufactured, a callous and reckless byproduct of capitalism and (settler) colonialism. This neglect is a feature rather than a flaw of racial capitalism, and it leaves the most vulnerable among us—poor, indigenous, black, brown, queer and trans, disabled, undocumented folks, children, incarcerated people, refugees, etc.—to fend for themselves. *California Fire & Water: A Climate Crisis Anthology* is a compendium of such voices, working to make meaning of their lives and futures amid ongoing climate crisis. Featuring some voices of the state's youngest poets, distinguished veteran writers, and those in between, this book is a soothing gesture of solidarity, an outstretched arm in the wake of helplessness that can befall those of us confronting the harsh reality of a planet engulfed in flames. How can we continue to navigate a life *in extremis*? We bring together our memories and cobble together our defenses—ancestral and contemporary, coalitional and creative—to ward off the fires, floods, earthquakes, tsunamis, and hurricanes that persist and shape our lives today.

SA Smythe
Tovaangar // Los Angeles basin
January 2020

Preface

I'm the kind of writer who's always responded to what's in front of me, whether it's child abuse memories or a fox eating persimmons in the front yard. When I saw a new grant that asked me to address something important to my community, of course I thought of wildfire. We were two months past containment of the Camp Fire in Paradise, California, 50 crow-flight miles away. The smoke had cleared. It was finally raining. People who'd lost their homes were starting to appear in our town because every domicile closer to Paradise had been rented.

If you don't experience a disaster yourself, it can be hard to imagine it. Photos and video are shocking, but they don't hijack your nervous system the way reality does. And they only last a few minutes. One thing I've learned about disasters is how far-reaching the consequences are and how long the effects last.

The grant wanted as much involvement as possible, especially with youth. That made me think of California Poets in the Schools, where I worked for 12 years as a new poet, teaching mostly in juvenile hall. Kids need to get their feelings out, and poetry can be the right conduit. I thought a lot, after the Camp Fire, about how those displaced children were doing, meeting for class in people's living rooms, playing basketball in unfamiliar gyms.

My county is small, rural, and white. The project seemed to me to need more reach, so I stepped beyond the borders of Nevada County, where I was Poet Laureate, and asked Cal Poets to send teachers everywhere they could. Fire is not the only trouble we're up against, so I broadened the lesson plan scope to include any kind of climate crisis our state has seen: floods, mudslides, smoke, drought, coastal erosion and sea level rise, refugee populations.

Again, in the spirit of reaching, I thought people would be moved and informed to read poems about climate crisis not just to write them. I know I am. So making an all-ages anthology on the subject and then donating it to libraries sounded useful, and organizing readings from the book to engage the public did too.

The teaching's been done, the poems were gathered from San Ysidro to Arcata, and you hold the result in your hand. I thought about Carolyn Forché's *Against Forgetting: Twentieth Century*

Poetry of Witness, a book that sustains me, as I put this one together. I bow deeply to the compilers who make a bouquet of many voices to show us ourselves: it's undervalued and important work. I send a nod also to Tim Green at *Rattle* and his idea that traditional vehicles for publication, with their multi-year lead times, aren't always fast enough to do justice to what's going in the world: sometimes poems need to be written and read in the same week.

The Academy of American Poets Laureate Fellowships were established to encourage and honor Poets Laureate. I wanted to pass on that recognition and include as many other California laureates as I could in the project. Some are hosting readings, some sent poems, some are cheering me on from the sidelines. I solicited work from Juan Felipe Herrera, who has been both our California and United States Poet Laureate, but the 13 current and 16 former county and city/town laureates included in these pages pretty much just showed up. There's even a migrant off-course: a relocated former Poet Laureate of the state Kansas.

People lose their homes for many reasons, not just climate-related. I live and work on the ancestral homelands of the Nisenan, that they never ceded. The house that Bank of America and I own together is a mile from the Nevada City Rancheria, the Nisenan reservation until their tribal status was terminated by the U.S. Government in 1964. It can be hard to know how to engage in personal reparations for the historic events from which we've benefited. I give respect, thanks, apologies, and money to the Nisenan whenever I can, and would like to acknowledge them here. Proceeds from the sale of this book will contribute toward their tribe of 147 members and federal restoration of their tribal status.

Climate crisis is an experience we are sharing. Thank you for your efforts so far on the planet's behalf. I encourage you, as I encourage myself, to keep imagining how to bring our skills and energy to bear in facing this new world and taking action.

Even writing poems can help.

Molly Fisk, editor
Nevada City//South Yuba watershed
January, 2020

WHAT TO SAVE FROM THE FIRE

Kim Addonizio

Grandma offed herself years ago
so that just leaves the Picasso
but it turns out to be a pencil drawing
you made at six, triangle of a sail,
one duck on a squiggle of water.
Up go the curtains in a bright rush.
You'd definitely save your daughter
and take her place on the pyre,
but she moved to a faraway island
after launching a few thousand ships.
Once you left a throw rug
on a floor heater to keep the darts
you were throwing from falling in
and woke to a room made of smoke,
but all that burned was the rug so
it didn't count, the way nothing counted
back then, you and your friends
carrying blankets and pillows outside to sleep
and opening all the windows. Fire is fed
by air, a slim lick of flame expanding
like most people in middle age.
What about your journals—
pages of proof you never changed
no matter what the mirror tells you.
Years from now someone might lick
the ink and taste snow, cheap wine,
the grilled cheeses you ate with your mother
at the Woolworth's counter.
Then again, look at those rosettes of self-pity
adorning the cake of your depression:
let the journals burn. Meanwhile
better wet a towel and hold it to your face.
Who's coming for you? Hopefully large men
in helmets and boots, and not a few students
exhuming a metaphor. Stay calm.
Throw darts. Some look like cruise missiles,
some like honeybees.

DEFYING FATE

Opal Palmer Adisa

They warned us
yes they did

But we refused
to listen

The location was
so beautiful

High above everyone
remote   peaceful

Our perfect get away
and it was for ten years

Now I wade through
ashes hoping to find

Evidence of a life lived
a future we had bargained on

CADAVER DOG

David Alpaugh

This was no playhouse but a house in earnest.
    –Robert Frost

A dog is barking in Paradise.
Sniffing scorched earth… hellish air.
His handler shouting urgently

"Over here!"

Man? Woman? Child? Metal prongs
thoughtfully finger suspect ash & soil;
rake up nothing but the mute remains

of a smart phone—plus all that's left
of a wedding ring (the diamond).
Nothing gold can stay.

Cadaver dog Gus's sense of smell
is 1000 times keener than yours
as he savors a scent so redolent

of all his masters search for—
that intimations of humanity
flood his canine heart and mind.

Shall this essence materialize?
Toss a ball or frisbee?
Share a strip of bacon?
Go for a ramble in the park?

"Good boy!"

How lovingly a dog has done what dogs
are taught to do; but minus tooth or nail
or bit of sullied flesh to bag for DNA—
man's best friend is left to grieve alone.

Not that there's time to howl.
Gus gets a pat on his head (but no reward).
The search party moves on.

DROUGHT SONNET

Lisa Alvarez

while waiting for the river to rise from its dry sleep
some stacked stone cairns taller than their children in its dusty bed
great fields of lupine bloomed blue in the parched margins
where the river once met the alpine lake

that fall acorns dropped early
impatient angry visitors knocking on roofs
white fibrous hearts splintered under foot
no blackberries no apples

great oaks dropped branches
on dreaming children below
her brother died in the last wet year
drowned face down on the river bank

where, as children, they launched
fleets of bark boats with sails of dry leaves

SONETO DE LA SEQUIA

(traducio por Luis Antonio Pichardo)

durante la espera para que el río se levante de su sueño seco
unos construyeron en su cama polvorienta hitos de piedra más
 altos que niños
grandes campos de lupino florecieron azul en los márgenes
 resecos
dónde el río en alguna vez se topaba con el lago alpino

ese otoño las bellotas cayeron temprano
vistantes impacientes y enojados tocando techos
corazones blancos y fibrosos se estallaron bajo pie
no moras no manzanas

grandes robles tiraron ramas
encima de niños soñando por debajo
su hermano murió en el último año mojado
ahogado boca-bajo en la ribera

dónde, cuando niños, lanzaban
flotas de barcos de corteza con velas de hojas secas

WHAT IS THE QUESTION?

Cynthia Anderson

The last of the human freedoms is to choose one's
attitude in any given set of circumstances...
–Viktor Frankl

Strong winds blow in from the backcountry,
bearing ash from a wildfire gone cold.
The fine gray haze obscures sky and sun,
proof that events we thought were over
follow us into the meditation loft
where we sit inviting our minds to be still.
Woodpeckers drill straight into the building,
backhoes beep from the service yard below,
loose metal flaps against the roof.
Vast questions like Why are we here?
shrink to How can we stand it?
Most eyes stay closed, willing to prove
that our minds can go blank for one second—
no matter how the world shocks us
or insists on uprooting our calm.

(UNTITLED)

Daniel Ari

How shocking to think, how discomfiting to feel
that after all that highway driving and air conditioning
and hairspray and bargain bin browsing that there would
after all be a cost we overlooked or sometimes pretended
to overlook or pretended to defer, that it would come due
and we would say, well, it's embarrassing, and fun
while it lasted, and I can't help but be cavalier in grief,
because what can I do now that it's too late to return
the clothes to the soil, the bees to the house,
the blue to the sky? I guess we guessed
we'd get away with it. How shocking to imagine
even the possibility, even enough to invite
right now the extra seconds to put the banana peel
in the green bin, rinse the peanut butter jar for the blue bin
and store the plastic bag for another use, another day.

THE HEAT AGAINST MY FACE

Quinn Arthur

If I were an owl.
I would fly fast
through the gray
silky willow trees at dusk.
I would watch the copper
colored stream flow
at sunrise. I would watch
a fox hunt rabbits at midnight.
I would soar through a
river with drips of water
passing my flapping wings.
I would even fly through
the burning fire in
the sizzling sun
with the heat
against my face.
The universe taught
me this bravery.

3rd Grade, Francis Scott Key Elementary School
San Francisco

FIRE AND RAIN

Lea Aschkenas

For Storm Thomas (October 27, 1958 – August 28, 2016)

When the rain wakes me
at that early hour,
no longer night
and not yet morning,
I think of you, my now-gone friend.

I measure your absence in seasons—
that first fall of endless rain and floods,
of mudslides and collapsing cliffs,
overflowing dams and evacuations;
the mountain trails we used to hike
blocked off before I could return, alone;
each "Storm Update" email alert
more cutting than cautionary, each
bringing me back to that first email,
the one that informed me
of your demise.

That second fall, wind storms
ripped through the mountains,
roared into residential zones,
left freeway-jumping fires in their wake.

All through that dry summer of your departure—
before the fire, before the rain—
you struggled to reinvent yourself,
wondering how far a man could fall,
how many mistakes he could make
before that initial spark inspiring change
would wane and, then,
snuff out.

Tonight the rain falls hard,
disrupting sleep, disturbing dreams,
washing away
last season's ashes.

"...AND THE BEAUTY IN FIRE"

Claire J. Baker

From a hilltop
the Santa Rosa horizon
blazes into the ocean,
spreads poppy meadows
toward the beach where we
build a driftwood fire, beneath
the chiming first stars,
a full moon rising,
overflowing
with borrowed light.

And we remember a flock
of flamingos flying
through a foothill forest,
flamboyant birds celebrating
a firestorm on California's
Paradise plateau,
where pioneer inlets and outlets
are now too few,
long paved over
and not wide enough.

We saw a dog waiting day and night
beside its family ruins.

AFTER THE FIRES

Devreaux Baker

We were afraid to go back
afraid to listen to the stories
ash and bone might tell
We wanted to believe our lives were immutable
untouchable by nature, fate or disaster
At twilight we skirted the base of the first burned hill
reclaimed her scorched shoulder
her ruined slope
The ground beneath our feet released puffs of smoke
like ancient ghosts they rose up around us
to disappear into wind
We thought of Spirit Lake in the mountains near Shasta
how some believe out of nothing a spirit may be reborn
into the physical shape of a tree, a bush, a rock or stream
Is this what your Grandmother felt the morning she called for
  the healer
to bring the spirit back into the shape of you?
How the healer came into your Grandmother's kitchen where
  you lay
and began to sing a song to reclaim your place among the living
There was so much loss you had to travel through
She told your Grandmother to make a circle of salt
to open all the windows
Is this what I have learned from you?
How the soul of a thing cannot be destroyed by fire but
remains buried beneath ash
bound in a circle of salt waiting to return
to its physical presence?
You returned through a dark land
with no sign posts, only spirit songs and the rattle of sacred bones
to guide you
You came into all four directions at once
and startled your Aunts who placed their hands
in a blessing on you
We stand at the base of the burned hill

and taste the left behind spirit of lightning
the soft core of ash, the outline of smoke
that haunts this body of earth
At the edge of the road one tree persists
like the spirit of a child
moving through a land of loss
into the body of a boy again
dreaming a new shape
into all four directions at once
returning to the land of his birth.

BREATH?

Sebastian Baker

I breathe in death
I breathe out love for this world
I breathe in sickness
I breathe out new life
I breathe in smoke
I breathe out warm cookies
I breathe in gas from cars
I breathe out melted chocolate
I breathe in pollution from oceans
I breathe out peace for the world
What do you breathe?

———

5th Grade, Arcata Elementary School
Humboldt County

DEAR FUTURE

Joan Baranow

Preliminary treatment uses screens or grinders to capture or macerate solids such as wood, Q-tips, and dead alligators so they don't muck up the works further down the line. —Dave Praeger

We tried, really. When ooze gooped up the ocean
we invented suction to separate plastic from salt,
but too many dolphins got torn apart in the process
and you know how we feel about dolphins.
After that Congress canceled the Internet
and put the country in reverse.
No one could remember bologna sandwiches
or Simon Says anymore anyway.
The Super Bowl, however, remained
high octane. We hosted parking lot brawls
and instantaneous T-shirts.
Not so Women's Lib weeping at the seams.
It all depends on what we thought was real.
Sidewalk cracks were avoided.
As were robo-calls. Even the thought
of lab animals patched up for the night.
We could never agree on which death
was best for the country. On whose terms.
Humans had become immune to irony.
We engineered nets to catch the suicides,
then legislated assisting them to death.
Please know these were the good days
before you replaced us. We thought
nothing of trading hearts among species,
injecting toxins to effect a cure, passing
the body through enormous magnets to map
the damaged gut.
It was good times. It was plenty
of packaged beef, bubble wrap, clam shell,
call waiting, deodorant, non-stop flights,
zero prime rate, Safe Zone training, and
antimicrobial copper-alloy surfaces

too slick to stick to, though
measles made a late comeback at Disneyland.
It was easy to get sweet on nature
with a bottle of amoxicillin in the fridge.
We stripped off the lead paint and installed seat belts.
We figured death happened to other people
for the best reasons. The worst, they say,
was picking Q-tips by hand out of
sewer grates. That was 10% of the job.
The rest was shoveling sludge from city drains.
As I said, despite being a bickering, tormented lot,
we tried. We really did.

GOD OF ROOTS

Ellen Bass

Meanwhile, the heat and light
of a flaming star rush
93 million miles to reach us,
baby girls are born
with their four hundred thousand
egg cells already formed, otters
keep grooming their guard hair, whirling
the water, working air into the deep
underfur, beluga whales swim
along the earth's magnetic field,
chicks pip a circle of holes counterclockwise
around the blunt end of their eggs,
pressing with their feet and
heaving with their shoulders,
larvae eat their way through the soft
mesophyll of oak leaves, leaving a trail
of dark feces in their wake, tart juice
swells within the rinds of lemons,
and under the earth the god of roots
goes on painting the lustrous fringe
with a brush so delicate—
only one sable hair—as though
there were all the time in the world.

HEAT

Ruth Bavetta

And the sun said,
let there be fire
and there was fire.
And the fire said,
let there be wind.
and the wind was throbbing
and the beast of the flames
pulled taut over the hills,
said naught to the chaparral,
and nil to the coyote.
And the coyote ran.
And the rabbits ran.
And the deer
and the rattlesnake
and the quail ran.
And the wind
sprang from its kiln
and tongue-licked the eaves
and the rafters
and the roof.
And the smoke
was air and the air
was smoke.
The air was our bodies.
It was our shadows
against the sky.

MORNING

Judy Bebelaar

It waits now, before birdsong,
a patient stillness.

It waits
for a sky full of music
as it was in the old dawns here,
waits for paired Monarchs,
trios, a winged kaleidoscope.

Waits for itself as it was
before DDT,
before Monsanto and monocrops,
before the plundered forests.

As after fire, green returns,
morning light holds possibility.

And that one Anise Swallowtail
my husband photographed
and framed,
yesterday's gift out of the blue,
says perhaps
it is not yet
too late.

BUT NOW TO FIRE

Mouad Belkhalfia

Once I was the mist in the clouds
I was the one drop of rain
But now I am the storm
But now to fire,
But now to smoke.

4th Grade, Cleveland Elementary School
Oakland

"GOLDFISH SURVIVE DEADLY WILDFIRES"

Henri Bensussen

Santa Rosa Press-Democrat Headline

Twelve goldfish found in a tub
swimming in the ashes of a wildfire
quenched two months past.

Fish manufactured like toys
given as prizes, pets, hypnotic
motion in a bowl. Golden spears

Flashy glide within a quart of water
expendable, not worth a vet. Give them
a frond of green and tiny castle

Pinch of food, a glance of care.
When ill that flash of gold turns
gray—as muted shades of ragged

Cart pushers living creekside
needy as these survivors
for just enough to stay alive.

ROOT CAUSE FAILURE ANALYSIS

Stella Beratlis

Define influx:
an arrival of or entry of large numbers of people
or an inflow of water into a river, lake, or the sea—

I am trying to tell you
all the ways a thing can go wrong,
how great blue herons are landing on
mats of soil and plants right now, in Sacramento slough—

no matter how many temporary
emergency influx shelters
are built to house the human overflow,

to manage the effects
of human devastation syndrome—

I am trying to tell you,
my love, we are tule berms--
created by years of peat moss
accumulation, dense tangle
of Delta weeds, our hearts
a weathered laydown in the sloughs

open, open to children
and yet can it get more
catastrophic?

the influx inevitable, and even approaching the task
from a multidisciplinary perspective:
the spaces where physics, soil, scars, fluids
and distortions intersect.

Loss is breaking our hearts.
Rising seas and powerful currents
tear the roots, wash the soil—

Oh everyone, I am trying to do this thing:
not limit my understanding
to the engineering environment—

instead, the root cause may exist
right here, where we refuse to allow
a great blue heron to walk
into our thicket of nerves
and change us.

HARD TO PLAN FOR

Gene Berson

Outside the tire shop waiting room
a sparrow underneath a faded Suburu
sips from a puddle of condensation
dripping from the air conditioner.
Smoke from the fires is everywhere.

"Have a seat." The young woman
behind the counter
takes care of business:
"I'll get'm right on it!"

The dude next to me into his phone
scrolls through pics with his expert thumb
an older lady across from me
fidgeting with the clasp on her purse
looks at me, her face full of appeal.
I smile, and look away.

The tire shop is full of the smell of new tires.
We have Coffee Mate and hunting magazines
as we wait, and are grateful to have made it
and not to be stuck on the side of the road.
I look out the window again.

The sparrow stays
in the shade under the bumper
her beak open for the heat
as if she's trying to sing.

THIS TIME

Claire Blotter

All   you have
   to do is read hear
     dried   crackling grasses
   now before
   they burst
into golden merciless
      flames

Then gather your box
  of important papers   pets
     devices and   head   for open
space before trees
   buildings crash down and around
      you thinking this is

    a movie really a drama
     a dream but it's

life now   your life
on this flooded burning planet

so many crowded together   flaming
        floating loose   inside

from anger greed and pride and this
    time   we   will
      not   escape
    suddenly

    this time   we must hear each   other
        or die

SUNDOWNER WIND

Laure-Anne Bosselaar

Three days now & the sundowner stubborn: a hot hiss
in the jacaranda. It's in bloom. There is no blue
    like this one, dusted by drought & dusk
                but flowering all it can—

raising its fists to the other blue — up there — sun-fraught,
    contrailed, hazed & exhausted with light, but there,
        unfailingly there.

The streets are empty, but for a mockingbird on a roof, he too
    doing all he can, singing to the scorched mountains
pockmarked by the Tea Fire.

The sundowner danced
        with that fire for days,
    its flames still a rage in my old friend's eyes:
    she lost all she had to it.

I think of her often, bent over, sifting
    pottery shards from her house's ashes & finding
    solace there. My god: solace—in so little.

The sun's down. The wind dies in the tree.
    I thumb the two wedding bands on my finger, have them
    do their little dance together: tiny rings
in a stillness that can't silence everything.

DRUID'S HALL, NORTH MARIN

Heather Bourbeau

She never understood the need to celebrate anything, including the end of deadly fires, with a barbeque. Instinct or hair of the dog? Like smokers on a hike, men gathered around the wood smoke paying gratitude to those who fought to save their homes, their lives. She had her potato salad and warm soda, far from the smell of burning. The fear and loss too raw to scar. She was grateful to be alive, to have these people, or she would be when she could feel again. For now, she allowed herself the quiet of shock, the numb of relief.

FIRE SEASON

Judy Brackett

I'm thinking about air caught
in pockets—arrested, ensnared,
N and O gases jostling,
warm, brown, wet air in halfcup
of morning's dark roast.

Or haze in closed-up house,
smoky, a different brown.
Or in runaway fires raging miles away
up forest canyons, the air there
red, hellish.

Hummingbird sips from red-petaled
blue-glass feeder, then perches
on potato rock on deck rail, then rises
to dip beak and drink, then perches,
then drinks in more cool blue and whirs up
and away, air and water warming,
thickening inside him
or her.

White hibiscus blossom, purple-hearted,
cradles smoky air. My lungs, too,
are browning,
air in my empty cup   gone,
air in that forest   beyond heat,
still angry, still red.

Last night from thinnest air,
an indifferent black sky shot stars,
hundreds of stars, heedless, random,
too cold for comfort.

REMEMBERING WATER

Katy Brown

Remember the world of water?
Emerald ponds,
aqua seas,
turquoise bays,
opal falls—

remember the meadows,
alive with garter snakes
and salamanders—

and the rain?
    gentle showers
    steely downpours
    virga that never reaches ground—

remember the world
alive with the sounds of
water in motion —

we will tell our grandchildren
about this world
on desert nights
under an arid moon.

FLAMENCO

Susan Browne

Because of the smoke, the sun is orange
as I walk around the shrinking lake,
the light casting a turmeric glow on my arms,
on everyone's legs in summer shorts,
on the chest of the shirtless man running
toward me, his shoes untied.

I worry he'll trip, but he seems unconcerned.
He carries an iPhone in one hand,
a stereo speaker in the other,
delivering a dance tune to the scorched air.

We want a song no matter what and heat
between bodies, sweat glittering like broken glass
along a collarbone, someone to flamenco with
at least for a few moments, laces flailing,
the burnt sky burning through us.

A flotilla of mallards glides by,
dipping green heads tinged tangerine
into the greasy water. The future visible
as a clavicle. Under the skin of smoke, lovers
lie on the shore, kissing like wildfire.

LEARNING ABOUT TREES

Kirsten Casey

Notice first, that they are tall, beyond
the power poles that bend and spark
under the weight of January snow.
The trees know their yoga, have stretched
and bowed only to return square shouldered,
in proper posture.

Please recognize the deep moles, blackened
by lightning strikes, in the thick bark
that was once sapling skin
now ragged and squirrel-abused, a home
and a maypole and a scratching post.

Most of the roots are hidden, bulging
wooden veins. They hold trees to the ground,
heavy, primitive ship anchors,
eventually rusting and rotting through.

When the trees are old enough they fall
because their insides are now beetles,
or the wind shifts to the north,
or there is not enough water,
or the late winter soil is too drenched
and has to let go.

You've already seen the diagram,
know the arrows' path, all of that oxygen
and carbon dioxide. And you've read
that slim green book about a boy
who sold his tree in pieces
and ended up old on a stump.

This isn't to warn you, but just to let you know,
that sometimes they outlive the people in their shade,
with their wide trunks and mysterious rings
and treetop perspective. Sometimes they burn,
cracking and shaking hands, in a bluster of sparks.
Sometimes people carve letters into them,
a scar they cannot read, in a language
that is not their own.

FIREBORN

Aileen Cassinetto

I once went wild
over repurposed things—
tweeds, beads, driftwood, silvery
wormwood got worked
into frames, footgear, chandeliers.
My favorite, though,
is a floor lamp from a limb
trimmed from an old manzanita,
the color of burnished red pear.
Wild child of the last wildfire,
evergreen and unsparing,
our gratitude for the little apples,
and the many equally
wild and resolute things
that fed on them—
that charm of hummingbirds,
that grist of bees,
that flutter of butterflies.
You were the kindling,
and the offering,
the timeworn prayer
above the movement of air.

IF FOUND, THEN MEASURED

Marcelo Hernandez Castillo

1.
Now that I can, I am afraid to become a citizen.
I don't want to become anything because I'm afraid of being seen.

I am arriving, and departing,
and later I will punish myself for looking over
at the person sitting next to me on the plane, checking their
    screen
and reading their email. For now there is no punishment.
Today I have realized everyone is just as boring as me.
Everyone in TSA had enormous hands.
I still refuse to travel with my green card.

2.
It is my mother's birthday and I bought her merchandise from a
    school
I didn't attend but only visited. She, too, understands the value of
    cultural capital.

Today I am wounded. I like to say wounded instead of sad.
    Sadness is reserved
for days when I can actually make money from what I do.
My mother raised me to make sure nothing I ever did I did for
    free.

3.
When I land, Northern California is burning.
We keep a suitcase near the door just in case.
A man calls me three different names before giving up
and asks if my son has begun coughing yet.
Beneath all that ash, no one seems bothered if you cry in public.

Sitting around a circle of grateful alcoholics, some of whom will
    leave
the room towards a clear portrait of their ruin,
which can either mean they will or will never return,

a man tells me I have been selfish, and I admit I have.
Sometimes I want every goddamn piece of the pie.

A woman pulls aside her mask to smoke and says
she's going to look up what temperature
teeth begin to melt, the implication being that if teeth melted,
they won't be able to identify her parents who are still missing in
    Paradise.

When I pray, I don't know who I am talking to yet.
I take the eucharist in my mouth for the first time
since changing religions and it is not as holy as I imagined.

4.
How easy. How effortless. This breath.
I'm here. I'm here. I'm right here. I want to say.
I wish things were simple, like taking just one drink
and not another, like not burning in a fire,
like letting things be good without being holy.
I wouldn't have to pretend to try
to resume the bounty of this blossom.

FIRE MIND

Brandon Cesmat

October firestorm rolls west over
the rim of Eden Creek Canyon.
Smoke from hundreds of homes, barns,
photos and lives of twenty-one neighbors
roils in incense of white sage
sacred to tribal people on two reservations
now ablaze, their outlawed spring burns
resurrected brutally in autumn.
Recognizing the ghost of smoke releases me
to accept losing everything so that when
our house emerges after fire, only planks of
patio aflame, I resist calling it "blessing."

That night, hot spots burn around canyon,
the only lights there until neighbors rebuild—
power lines burned like fuses,
exploding suburbs in the brush—
and above spot fires, stars
calling back thousands of others, dark insisting.

The second day after fire, I walk the rim,
first time in twenty years. Consoling neighbors
I'd never met as they sift ashes over concrete foundations,
I trespass freely to the east,
catch five goats, two pigs, a cat with
burnt paws. I shoot two horses without hooves,
their lungs singed, the blood they breathed
the only moisture within miles. I shoot
into another mind that becomes mine.
The fire: the rifle, and my hand: the bullet.
I follow a trajectory heartless as flames over so many.

Next week at a funeral, people flow through my arms.
I survive to hold them, open my cage of ribs.
Their sobs become my heartbeat, their tears: my blood.

My warmth from pressure of motion,
the same heat Santa Anas raise crossing The Mojave.
The town weeps itself dry while I wonder,
where are my tears of survival?

Each March, I burn brush. The flame at
the matchtip, the shape of an orange tear.
Neighbors watch. Every spring a warning.

FIRE HAIKU

Teresa Mei Chuc

my heart
the Santa Ana winds today
branches fall to the ground

ON THE ANNIVERSARY OF A FIRESTORM

Susan Cohen

Not one? My mother on the phone.
Not one wall, not one floor.
Not one painting left?

Not one chimney, not one plate.
How to draw a picture of not.
The news says tongues of flame,

but a firestorm has teeth
that bite and grind to grit, a hunger
galloping like Cossacks.

Their neighbor
who didn't know they were away
hammered their door with fists

and shouts before she fled
to save herself, the road
a tunnel through flames,

people stumbling downhill
while swatting cinders
that smoldered in their hair.

We send my parents photos
to prepare their homecoming.
Then back to the work of not

finding anything to find.
My mother hopes just one
fill-in-the-blank survived.

She begs relatives to replace
her shoebox full of snapshots
each penciled on the back

with names and dates, proof
of faces once attached
to the voices in her thoughts.

Some mail her images bled to brown,
likely to dissolve in daylight, but
the generation's frail, they forget

who's who—details lost, the way fire
swallows cars, licks the color off,
spits out only frames of steel.

On the street where their house stood:
puddles of pure aluminum,
congealed; and a fleet

of gutted cars waist-high, bumps
in the new landscape, tires
bitter in the air we breathe.

My mother wishes she had given
me the samovar, regrets
denying that footstool to a niece

who loved its childhood perch
visiting our Nana: its bowed-legs
of mahogany, pink needlepoint

of blossom on the cushion top's
deep green. My mother accepts
fire as chastisement. Fire—

the sternest parent—chides her
not to cling. Yet, she wishes.
Are you sure there's not just one...

For days we hunkered
on foundation walls, sifting with a screen
what was my parents' house

and then was not. The ashes, warm
at first, granted us a few fused coins,
earrings melted into mass, shears

crusted with something else
that had swapped atoms
for ash. Ash coated us

till we were colorless,
blanketed us with stillness
that begged not to be disturbed.

As we sieved for anything
complete enough to tell
its story of survival,

we could see for blocks where
others also bent, knee-deep
in ash, and excavated silence.

HOW TO READ THE SUMMER SKY

Jessica Cohn

I miss the Washington cherries already,
can't eat them fast enough,

sucking sweet flesh off each pit,
spitting stones and stems into a handheld bowl.

The late summer bleeds cherry,
raspberry, apricot, fig, plum.

Such trespass—avocados, artichokes, green grapes,
baby lettuces. A heavy basket, and never thanks enough.

It's late in the season, when we take our comforts
in blue ribbon apples, world's biggest pumpkins,

a harvest of pies at the county fair.
Everything on a stick because that's how we like it.

So late, when the nights mock an orange sun, give us starless
 night skies
we do not recognize. Our norths run out.

In tinder hills, metal raptors circle dry sacrifices of scrub oak
 and thistle.
The hottest month ever, swooping ever so slowly.

Slack glaciers and sea ice, slip their watery noose down. In Iceland,
the people dedicate a plaque to Ok, the first glacier gone.

And what of us? What can be done? Perhaps, we leave lavender offerings.
Perhaps, plant for bees, bidding, Come back. For to whom

much is given. The Perseids, in retreat as summers end. A meteor is just
a piece of sand in motion. It has no answers.

But we can wish. Oh, how we wish.

TELL YOU WHAT

Brad Crenshaw

Tell you what, the air aloft is falling.
Here it is, October, November, people
on the mountain speak again about
hydraulic jumps and fires. The power is

already down. Personally, I'm on
the wharf in Santa Cruz, but even so
I'm listening for downslope winds beginning
high before descending in a sinking

train of music aiming overland
and tumbling toward me on the coast. I take
a lung-full in, sampling for smoke
arriving from Sonoma. All of us

are breathing it. If I were to die
and then return to earth as horses, running
with the speed of money, I would fly
the flames behind me flaring into canyons,

sweeping through the prehistoric fuels
and towns to overtake the traffic trapped
on chains of roads as conifers exploded
overhead. Are they beautiful,

these evergreens ringed in elemental
force? Wreathed demonically? A problem
I will leave unsolved. If I chose
a bird, I'd be a phoenix to come out

alive and recognized on thermals rising
over vineyards and incendiary
homes. Really, I'd be chasing safety
same as residents evacuating

underneath the haze and rain of soot
to reach as refugees the temporary
camps popping up, and populating
open spaces. Lanterns sparkle here

and there. Someone lucky saved his ass
when chaos drafted every buoyant
movable alive, and separated
friends and families. Circumstances

fly apart so fast. Fathers on
their dying phones are calling children still
on route. Sisters hold out hopes for detours
full of serious grace, which I'm here

to say are unattainable in country
currently alight, and commonly
reset in violent conflagration. Such
derision drives us all to ground.

THE DAY THOMAS WAS BORN

James Cruz

With one single spark
Your life began
You tremble
Fragile
But slowly, as you grow
Stronger
You burn and blaze brightly,
Warming my frozen fingers
Your constant crackling
Clears the comforting quiet

———

11th grade, Pacific High School,
Ventura

WILDFIRE AFTERMATH PHOTO

Doc Dachtler

*1221 F
(aluminum melts)*

On the ground
from under the hood
of a burned out car,

a large puddle
of hardened,
pooled silver.

A body there
would have burst
into flames.

AFTER THE PEDDLERS DISAPPEARED

Amy Elizabeth Davis

I bundle torn clothes, but the ragmen
have stopped stopping by. No horses
with carts bring milk or come to sharpen

knives. A different coast, a century turned,
and the voice of a grandchild all push history
further back. Once, bad fiction told us

the churning planet would split this coast
from the continent, send its collapsed geology
into the Pacific. Now, we reasonably expect

water to come ashore, splay over lowlands,
& push deeper into the interior. Yet maybe not.
Perhaps our doom will not arrive with rising oceans

after all. We thought this winter would go thirsty.
But up & down the block, ark frames sprout
in yards. Rain feeds brush that quilts mountains

with tinder, ready to explode when drought
& lightening next mix. After fire season, denuded
slopes will launch mud, & mud will rip houses

from foundations. The room grows chill. Wheels
slosh beyond the windows. Dirt & rock travel
in small amounts, not just by landslide. Perhaps

the storm drains that open onto every street
will carry the hills, by grain & pebble, into the water.
California will trickle into the tide. Rain will wash us

& wash us away. The sky turns up the volume.
I find an outgrown sweatshirt in the pile headed
for recycling, drape its skateboard insignia

across my cold shoulders. I must caulk, buy wipers.
Puddles spread & rise. Tomorrow, toadstools
will cover the lawn. I might need new boots after all.

WILDFIRE

M.J. Donovan

She feels the char of worry
on the back of her throat
like smoke,

And like the smoke,
she swept
down the valley
toward the sea
seeking sanctuary by the coast,

But even here the hills disappear
into that russet-grey
of California on fire.

Her baby, not yet born,
rests heavy,
feels the pulse of
soot-tinged blood,
registers a quickening
in her breath.

She stands near the edge
of the sea cliff,
longs for the breeze
to sweep away her fret,
prays to the Pacific
to pull in the rain.

The sea only lulls
in and out.
The sun low,
dragon-fruit red,
reflects metallic pink
pools around the kelp beds,
ribbons on the backs of waves.

MATH OF THE LOST WORLD

Linda Dove

One day, that color blue on the swallowtail
wing disappears. It had looked like metal

and powder at the same time, the color of a gun
that might bloom. Another day, it's a frog

or a spider, or it's the spider inside the frog—
so hidden, we can't see what we've done.

When the final male white rhino goes,
the caretaker is holding its ear in his hand

as if he is holding a coin—something he doesn't want
to lose. Is the ear the last piece of body to go?

Does he mean to help it along or hold it back?
In other words, what is the price of our attention?

We have loved every pine tree to a brown torch,
choked the oceans with straws drawn from our lips,

packed the scree with our prints. Body counts.
We say we prefer that the losses not add up, reckless

wad of paper here, zygote there. Disaster is a multiplier
like flies or rubber tires. Let us see the bee

collapse on the concrete, the polar bear go slack
like a sail, the fire reduce the parrots

to a green flame. Let the loss seem intimate,
or else, the harm is as far away as hands

cut from limbs. Just like that, we will be left
with paper tigers and a whale of a story.

IT'S SO HOT, I'M GETTING STUPID

Kim Dower

It's so hot, I just opened a can of tuna
with my teeth. I forgot there were can openers
was surprised to taste the fish oil mingling
with my blood, open cuts on my lips and mouth.
We'll do things under extreme conditions: step inside
of horses when we're freezing, fall in love with murderers.
I would kill for you, I tell my children. And, I would.
I have made bad decisions today in the heat.
I climbed the pole outside my window hoping
for a breeze. When I fell onto the moving car
the driver and I locked eyes before I tumbled off.
I am not dead. I am having lunch. A bowl of cream.
The driver is traveling north: strands of my hair
plastered onto his windshield.

ECHO

Cheryl Dumesnil

How can I help?
she asks again,

but the canyon
is filled with ash.

SPRING AS ADVERSARY

Kate Dwyer

Mid-month it rained so hard
the daffodils lay down and did not get up again.
The apple trees pelted us with blossoms;
death by wet confetti.
I emptied the rain gauge 6 times in 3 weeks.
And a sinkhole the size of a battleship
swallowed the parking lot at the tire store.
It took no prisoners.
Still, after 5 years of drought,
we dared not complain.
I put on my rain suit for the 64th day in a row
and tried to be grateful that
I would be soaked through before
the dog walk was over.

GRAY

Johanna Ely

Once I thought I understood
the color gray and all its nuances—
a wet, foggy blur of rain on glass,
a single, clear tear on the cheek,
a dull winter sky before snowfall.

Now I inhale it—
breathe the ashes that rise up
from charred squares of land
where houses once stood,
from drifting, swirling bones
that cannot speak.
My lungs fill with smoky air—
with particles of loss
that settle into gray dust,
into this new grief.

BAD CHILDREN

Gail Entrekin

Everywhere the planet
is pulling in her generous green
folding it up forever in the vast trunk
of history. She is taking down the curtains
of rain and giving them away to someone
in another dimension who will treat
them gently, she is rolling up
the atmosphere with its cigarette holes
and moth-eaten diatribes and when
she has packed her bags and slammed
the door and left us looking at each other
in silent shame, like bad children,
we will say, We didn't do it.
It was someone else.

PARTICULATE MATTER

Molly Fisk

If all you counted were tires on the cars left in driveways and
    stranded beside the roads.
Melted dashboards and tail lights, oil pans, window glass, seat
    belt clasps.
The propane tanks in everyone's yards, though we didn't hear
    them explode.

R-13 insulation. Paint, inside and out. The liquor store's plastic
    letters in puddled
colors below their charred sign. Each man-made sole of every
    shoe in all those closets.
The laundromat's washers' round metal doors.

But then Arco, Safeway, Walgreens, the library — everything
    they contained.
How many miles of electrical wire and PVC pipe swirling into
    the once-blue sky:
how many linoleum acres? Not to mention the valley oaks, the
    ponderosas, all the wild

hearts and all the tame, their bark and leaves and hooves and
    hair and bones, their final
cries, and our neighbors: so many particular, precious,
    irreplaceable lives that despite
ourselves we're inhaling.

BEFORE THE FIRES

Mary Fitzpatrick

Everything regrets its loss

In the growing bowl of day
an oak forest rises around me.

This is the hour when

the wish for rain, the tops of dreams
and the land that crackles and spreads

converge like tomorrow's calamities.

Here the hedgerows shrink
        as birdlets lift and scatter.
Here the tiny animals scratch
        in their long, divided cage.

And here something happens
beyond description or commentary...

While acorns and feijoas fall
        with tiny thud or clatter,
one can't miss
        the oceanic roar

of traffic on 210
that rises with the sun

and is the sound of metal speed
brought by desert wind.

INTO THE THUNDER

Casey FitzSimons

Its self-made wind cracks trees. In its din
it drowns the thin patter of falling cinders.

The dog whines, claws clattering. You cough,
crouch, hold your breath. Your fright

becomes my dread, a thing so elemental
no water could possibly relieve it, a chthonic force

belonging to nature. It is not thought, but this deep loathing
of palpable, pervading horror that will not be quenched.

My pictures singe and curl. My walls and pages tear and crum-
ble,
dissolve to silt. My speeches hiss and fizzle, finally pop.

Opposed across a chasm of what I do not want,
will not have, refuse to be reconciled to, cannot be rid of,

fire and water roar, do away
with all I thought I would remember.

FIRE!

C.B. Follett

Air thickens with the burn of trees.
Rufous clouds sheet the sun
and drop the temperature.
Our eyes grow rough and somewhere
out of sight, trees are dying
broadcasting seeds
in an artillery of flame.

For five days southwest winds
have carried news that fire
is winning. Acres blacken
towns cringe and scatter their inhabitants
like buckshot carrying baby pictures
and Aunt Mary's Wedgewood teapot.

Animals are long away.
Sniffing up heat and danger
they snap their tracery
down slopes, downwind,
urging their young.

Insects and snakes slide below ground
or retreat into the pith hoping
for cooler air.

When the fire passes or quells
they slip out into filtered sunlight.
Animals work their way back
and like film run in reverse, people
return to see what has been left them.

Earth-char offers little shelter
from cold, few protections
from predators but soon,
long before the smell has rolled off,
green things
fastened hard to the soil
will reach up
and start again.

A CAUSE FOR WORRY

Leonardo Fusaro

Don't worry child, it will be all right
the world is on fire with artificial light
as smoke plunges countries into endless night
and some wonder who we should really fight
Don't worry child, it will be okay
even though chemicals turn the swaying grass grey
and while polar bears run and play
some wonder if they can even have one more day
Don't worry child, you'll be just fine
though we wonder why corporations continue to mine
away at a planet, once green with oak and pine
but now some wonder if we crossed the line
There is a cause to worry child, it may not be all right
the forest blaze with a fire too bright
the haze of ash is clouding air sight
and now we all wonder if we've killed ourselves with this blight

10th grade, Pacific Community Charter High School
Mendocino County

FIRES ALL AROUND

Mary Gast

Varnish,
Flecks of prom dresses,
Pine needles, gun powder, book bindings,
PCBs, celery stalks, and rabbit fur
Hashed into the haze we breathe,
That dyes the rising sun
A neon tangerine.

LUNA LLENA EN VERANO DE SEQUIA

Rafael Jesús González

La luna llena se eleva
con un tinte rojizo
      del humo
de los bosques encendidos.
En la sequía las aguas
que levantaría
      se escasean
como el salmón en los ríos.

Su color, al aparecer,
es ese del perturbo
      en la sangre.

FULL MOON IN A DRY SUMMER

The full moon rises
with a reddish tint
      from the smoke
of the forests burning.
In the drought, the waters
she would lift
      grow scarce
as the salmon in the streams.

Her color, it would seem,
is that of the disquiet
      in our blood.

ONE SMALL DEATH

Taylor Graham

for Mike

You can't help turning the talk
to wildfire, your son hotshot firefighter

back from the big one. *Which
big one?* You brush the question off

like a spark. Your boy's hotshot crew
filing through moonscape ash and char.

A buddy kicks a blackened stone
out of the way

but it's no stone, it's charred alive,
just breathing.

Burned raccoon, not moving.
Your son tells his buddy,

End it with your Pulaski.
The buddy can't make himself do it.

So your son kills it.
But that can't kill it in his brain,

he has no choice but to tell
you. And you tell me. The beast, dying

lives third-hand, charred in my
brain. It wants to be told.

FROM THE FOREST, BURNING

Cleo Griffith

Hyacinths whisper
like a swarm of docile blue bees
within a motion too fragile
to be called wind.
Crickets ease under the drapes of ivy.
The sun, low, wears garnet
spread out in folds, a regal cape
edged in diminishing hues.
Blue-gray smoke
unrolls its gauzy yardage
across the valley,
bunching at the bottoms
of the foothills.
Fragrance not unpleasant
in its dilution by distance
teases the nostrils of the calico cat
astride the fence.
The temperature of the barriered air
drops a few degrees
denying the heat so far away
where trees are crying.

CLIMATE CHANGE FEARS OF FIFTH GRADERS

Group poem

Fear of the next ice age
Fear of losing my cat
Fear of having more panic attacks
Fear of dying
Fear of a tsunami
Fear of tornados
Fear of a hurricane
Fear of losing people I love
Fear of losing something
Fear of losing my brother
Fear of running out of resources in the world
Fears of fear
Fears of death
Fear of losing my family
Fear of the world ending
Fear of running out of food and water
Fear of losing my house
Fear of being trapped by horses
Fear of being killed in my sleep
Fear of getting burned from a fire
Fear of losing my life
Fear of being trapped
Fear of being overwhelmed
Fear of running out of oxygen
Fear of freezing to death
Fear of the greed of people
Fear of what I can't help with
Fear of running out of time
Fear of pain
Fear of my family dying
Fear of dying by drowning
Fear of and a lot more
Fear of losing my best friend
Fear of losing the people I love
Fear of me not seeing my grandma again

Fear of the dark but with scary noise
Fear of losing everyone and being by myself
Fear of losing my house
Fear of being boiled alive
Fear of losing a collection of something
Fear of the ozone layer popping
Fear of the sun blowing up
Fear of pollution
Fear of the moon colliding into earth
Fear of the earth being shot out of orbit
Fear of our galaxy being swallowed by a black hole
Fear of natural disasters
Fear of being wasted
Fear of being buried alive

The 5th grade, Hidden Valley Elementary School
Santa Rosa

THE DROUGHT HAPPENED

Junior Gutierrez

the drought happened
it stopped raining
the aquifers dried up
      since there was no
    water
there were no crops
     and since no crops
     no food
     and no food nothing
to eat for
animals and nothing
to eat for humans
everyone was starving
the drought went on for
many
       years

5th grade, Selma Herndon Elementary
Livingston

THESE STONES

Lara Gularte

After the "Camp Fire" Paradise Pines, California

I follow behind a backhoe, see the burnt scarring,
a desolate landscape of ash heaps, vanished lives.

In a vacant lot of cinder, I remember my mother's Camellia tree,
how she liked Gerbera daisies, my grandmother's tea rose.

Granite binds me to this property, the stones
my uncle gave to my father, to stabilize the embankment.

I choose to believe something still breathes here.
When I call out, I hear a heartbeat.

Fierce rocks pull away from the ground,
and I remember who I am.

These stones on the hillside cover a stubborn root,
a long vein, blood of my blood, alive deep inside.

In the passage of my remaining days I'm here to survive myself,
grow wings to fly through smoke.

THEY SAY YOU LOST EVERYTHING

Lynn M. Hansen

for brother Dave and Karen

When an inferno races
one football field a second
through Paradise,
your classroom remains.

When a forty-foot wall of flame climbs
each side of your corridor of escape,
hot coals burning your tires,
a newborn granddaughter awaits you.

When your eight mules, obedient
despite crackle, boom, whoosh of fire
trust you and crowd into a four-horse trailer
now live in Redding.

When thirty-one pair of snowshoes,
a life of photographs, antiques,
harnesses are ash,
one freight wagon and your costumes survive.

When your church, textbooks,
home, barns, fences, landscaping
become a moonscape,
you and Karen are not lost.

For you, what remains,
is everything.

IMPERMANENCE

Katherine Harar

When the fire came to my house
it took everything but a copper bell
the flames swallowed its wooden tongue.

●

My neighbor's Buddha didn't burn
it watched over the char, the vacant land
and skeleton trees
eyes half-closed.

●

Flesh of books
ligaments of tables and chairs.
Mark's paintings.
He died two years after they did.

●

I knew then I couldn't belong
to the pines, the oaks and madrones
sun-smells of summer
long dry evenings alone.

●

Yesterday we smelled a new fire
as we drove in our un-melted cars
hundreds of miles from the flames.

●

In my tidy kitchen
I slide open a drawer, finger
a neat pile of folded dish towels.
Sniff the air.

PRIORITIES

Cynthia Haven

On the Williams Wildfire in the Sierra Nevada foothills

The flakes of flame fall soft as snow—
The anti-winter's fever heat
Is rising still. The fire-flakes glow.
And farther off, a golden sheet

Approaches us, adagio.
Behind it— wind, a blackened scene.
Inferno's gaudy sequins sow
The scorching air's acetylene.

Unriddle, sphinx, the force that flings
Such sky-borne terror in the night—
Above, daimonic music rings
The decibel that drives our flight.

A quick, last look inside—the spread
Of books and papers argues, "Stay."
Remain for labor, hearth, and bed—
We leave our bodies just that way.

Renounce Lot's woman, dying for
A life that fled her false retreat.
Turn the key gently. Lock the door.
Obey the darkness and the heat.

FOR CLAY

Willow Hein

Cusp of autumn, brown,
no relief of yellow aspen
or red maple.
Fires rage and still no sign of you.

Sequestered indoors, escaping
smoke and ash,
she paces.
Sleeps in fits and starts,
hip aching,
back spasming,
carrying the weight of you.

I dream of your entry
bringing the rain.
Watery womb holding the depths
bursting forth change,
water rising like a tide.

Cool liquid — sweat, tears, torrents —
finally sating King Fire,
who gobbles up the river canyon
in great plumes of greed.

You'll slip into this world, no trumpets sounding.
Only the miraculous opening of her pelvis,
bones rearranging themselves,
blood red sunrise.

Gush of moisture
into parched earth.
The ultimate act of faith.

All I can do is hold you
in this swirl of smoke and ash.

IT CAN BEGIN WITH CLOUDS

Juan Felipe Herrera

it can begin with clouds how they fray how they enter
then how they envelope the earth
in a second or two they vanish you
touch them they take you you find yourself in their absence
sometimes you read them somehow
the separation the losses the sky yes
it is the sky they were talking about the character for sky
you are there now
you have always been there now
where there is fire and
thunder-face behind the torn universe you can see this
how its shreds itself so you can see this that
is all there is then
nothing again then you again and the clouds
come to you and you pass.

HOW TO SPEND A BIRTHDAY

Lee Herrick

Light a match. Watch the blue part

                              flare like a shocked piñata

               from the beating
               into the sky,

                              watch how fast thin

wood burns & turns toward the skin,

the olive-orange skin of your thumb

                           & let it burn, too.

Light a fire. Drown out the singing cats.

Let the drunken mariachis blaze their way,

streaking like crazed hyenas

over a brown hill, just underneath

a perfect birthday moon.

GREEN FIRE

Donna Hilbert

My brother says he fears
the fire, since rain
has come and sun-burnt
hills seethe green
in shrub and flower.
I've heard the tales,
but never seen
the flash of green at sunset.
I strain for faith
in what remains unseen.
If it's true that each
contains the seed of other,
then I too expect to see
the fire burn green.

AFTER THE FIRES,,, IN THE MOUNTAINS,,,

Brenda Hillman

The spirit seedlings do their yellow best.
    The sister seedlings move to the cold ground;
they join the feral mother
dressed in ash.   They join the feral
brother dressed in ask ;;;
......///°··.

There came a time attached
to the cold ground. Golden-crowned.
Agencies moved humans to new
metal boxes. Flies on
    corpses of the question marks.
      Fucking stupid leaders—excuse me,
stupid fucking leaders said profit hotel
attack mode. Earth said,
the large gods are lucky
      not to exist. Unimaginable
        conflict as families apply for
          little scraps of state money.

At solstice, without despair,
when nights are long, we study
the classics that halt in the middle
of action. Humans loved life very much,
it was never just us vs. the sun king
or single minutes vs. all of eternity.

after SEM

LET THEM NOT SAY

Jane Hirshfield

Let them not say: we did not see it.
We saw.

Let them not say: we did not hear it.
We heard.

Let them not say: they did not taste it.
We ate, we trembled.

Let them not say: it was not spoken, not written.
We spoke,
we witnessed with voices and hands.

Let them not say: they did nothing.
We did not-enough.

Let them say, as they must say something:

A kerosene beauty.
It burned.

Let them say we warmed ourselves by it,
read by its light, praised,
and it burned.

THE DIFFERENT FACES OF FIRE

Henry Hoffman

Fire ripping, tearing, killing, the dying fading forest
As the fire grows you can hear squeals and cries, as animals retreat
Squirrels running, birds flying
Ants crackling up in the air smell like burnt sap as the forest dies

That shiver you get when the cold house starts freezing
You realize how much you need fire
Fire scars and tares the cold apart
You feel that warm sensation
You feel protected like you have a shield in a battle
You feel strong and powerful
You hear
the crackling of the fire, see it dancing
That warm happy face of fire

Fire is little, fire is big, fire is dark, fire is bright.
Fire has many faces—hate, love, happiness
Many die, many live because of fire

You may love something, and you may lose it in the flames
But there's still hope for a new love, a new life,
And a hope for more and more in the face of fire

4th Grade, Lu Sutton Elementary School
Novato

THE TREE

Jackleen Holton

They lived in my neighborhood.
The fire wouldn't even come close.
But there they were on TV, cutting down
the lone oak tree in their gravel-scaped
front yard because the flames might leap
from the branches to the shingled roof
of their rented duplex. The woman spoke
to the camera of their preventive industry
while her grown son, sweating into a red
bandanna, sawed away at the regal oak.
And some long-forgotten anger
smoldered inside me. I don't know why,
thirteen years later, I'm thinking about them.
It wasn't even a eucalyptus, all parchment and oil,
like the one that shaded my porch, the one
that would most certainly go up before
their thick oak took a light. But the fire
never even jumped the highway.

Today, the canyon's green from all the winter rain.
My mother just left after staying with us
for a week. I told my husband not to ask,
but of course he did. I really didn't want to know
how she voted. I said that my friend Caroline
reduced this whole mess to a handful of words:
The Russians tricked the rednecks.
And my mom winced a bit at that, the way
I used to shrink when she'd pick me up from school
in the old Monte Carlo with no right fender.
On TV, a man's being dragged off a plane,
and the bombs we knew would drop are dropping now.
There's a kernel of meanness in my heart today, a resurrected
rage, though I can't trace back this thought to where
it forked off to those yokels looking down at a pile
of felled branches, their job half-done—

the handsaw wouldn't cut the trunk—
but they knew a guy who'd loan them a power saw
to bring down what was left of the tree.

DREAMING OF FIRE

Twyla Hoshida

1. I am the embers of a flame
From the wind I learned to spark
like a star when the breeze blows
The wind taught me to move
like a flash of lightning
to move and burn the grass
When I move, I dream of fire
spreading throughout the land.

2. I am the storm
destroying everything
blowing over the earth
like a colossal fan at top speed
twirling my fingers through the clouds
kicking off water like an angry beast
I am destruction.

4th Grade, Cleveland Elementary School
Oakland

AFTER THE FIRE

Jodi Hottel

Though much is taken, much abides.
—Alfred Lord Tennyson

Some of what we lost
and some of what remains
can be named and counted,
but what emerges over time

is that some of what remains
was not apparent in our grief
and emerged only with time,
distance and birdsong.

Not apparent in our grief
was the returning rain,
birdsong in the distance, and
what had been hidden by ash.

The returning rain washes
shards of pottery, reveals blades of green
that were hidden by ash—
spurring us to reassemble life.

Shards and greenery that
can be named and counted,
start to resemble a life and
some of what we thought was lost.

TWO FLAMES

Michael Hughes

The flames were like a rainbow of red,
orange and yellow dancing on the trees.
They stay
away from the water so they
won't die down.
Fire is a destroyer ready to burn anything in its path.
The fire burnt the whole neighborhood.
Nothing but
flames and the smell of burnt oak remained.
If you go near it, you die.
The animals are gone, even my dog Frank.
Fire has taken the whole town.
Everything I know and love is gone.
How did we get through those flames?
I felt so scared of it.
Though it is
deadly, it is still beautiful.
Fire warms you up on a winter day.
Fire heats up your food.
Fire is two things—
Bad and Good.

———

4th Grade, Lu Sutton Elementary School
Novato

LOVE IN A TIME OF FIRE

Maureen Hurley

Some blamed the hot Santa Anas
while others cursed the Diablo winds,
howling at 75 miles an hour.
Whatever you call it, a maelstrom
devoured Santa Rosa de Lima's namesake.
The city is blanketed in a layer of ash
so a friend left red roses on all the cop cars.
What else was there to do in a time of fire?
We became the light in a darkened land.

(UNTITLED)

James Lee Jobe

The rain gutters are full and rushing,
And the water spouts are gushing
Like the overflow to a dam
On a very full lake.
The sky is even darker to the west,
Yet another storm is coming,
A follow-up to this one;
A hard right cross following a left jab.
This fight could go on for hours.

I AM THE ASHES

Leeloo Johansen

I am the ashes of the flames
From the wolf I learned to howl like fire
When the fire burns, the flames grow.
The fox taught me to run like a waterfall
When I sleep I dream of volcanoes and flames.

4th Grade, Cleveland Elementary School
Oakland

WHEN THINGS START TO BREAK

Tim Kahl

Two days after the big fire burns houses
and bodies by the score and the power company
reports an outage at the location where it starts,
the big investors begin to divest.
Oh Capital, my Capital, no longer are you
such an intrepid beast. Where is that will that tamed
a million acres of rain forest just last week?
You are the cat chasing after the laser dot
on the carpet. You are the friend during good times
who hears someone calling in the other room
when risk appears. All this time I was only
looking for you to be someone I could have
a few beers with. I wasn't asking for much,
but it looks like the American dream is made
of much grander and more glittery stuff.
In my American Dream last night I found
myself in a place a lot like Europe,
the passenger trains running full from
Seattle to Denver to Kansas City, the stations
at the terminals brimming with life.
But you haven't built that dream yet,
have you, Capital? You haven't even gotten
around to dedicated bike lanes throughout the city.
Goddamnit, Capital, I've bought all that crap
you said I needed and now you do me like this?
You're just a little boy who makes bad choices,
then runs away when things start to break.
Bang! And they're off . . . look at all those
fledgling dollars setting out for the Cayman Islands,
The Isle of Man, Panama, the Bahamas, Dominica,
Nevis, Vanuatu, Costa Rica, Guernsey, Jersey,
Malta, Aruba. Oh, the places you'll live
safe from anything terrible ever happening to you.

END OF DAYS

Maxima Kahn

At first the day is spacious without power, clocks
stopped, sun bright, action
stilled, the autumn
halted in its falling.
No wind, though wind was predicted, the reason
the electricity was shut down. Light
over everything. Shadows
cast by fallen leaves. Shadows
in the mind being swept
one by one. A planetary feeling
or failing. The nearest creek
only a mile and a half.
We could walk for water, carry our
jugs as of old. I think
about Armageddon, meaning the end
of the power grid, the internet, this way
of life. I think about sharing my own
words, about Frederick, the mouse poet,
how he was needed
in the dark, cold days.
I think about the end of ambition
and find a stream flowing
through my mind.
But where will we get food? Every other problem
I think I can solve
with simplicity, a hole
dug for a toilet, the fire pit for warmth.
The gazania are still blooming
keen, orange-maned faces, though the garden
is covered in shadow.
And a deeper shade is falling.

FIRE SEASON

Susan Kelly-DeWitt

Driving home from the ocean—foam
coils like lacy sand dollars pasted to the wet
shore, fog banks boogie boarding in
with the evening surfers—we see
smoke clouds, sooty sky-islands
in the distance; wildfire tides
rolling toward us from the dry valley
grasses, parched hillsides.
I think of the caddis flies, midges, leafhoppers,
the snout moths, the click beetles—the swallowtails
and mourning cloaks; of the wolf and the recluse,
the orb-weavers, silk slingers,
all those non-human universes exploding
into flame—how we breathe them in, how
they drift into our lungs on wisps of char
vapor, while firefighters try to hold
the line and evacuated humans wait
in uncertainty's wings. Some days I feel
our aging hearts could be seen as dry umbels
of drought-stressed sweet fennel,
as spikelets of quaking grass or brome.

FIRST RAIN

Terri Kent-Enborg

If you're anywhere north
of Sacramento, turn down
Netflix and Spotify.
Turn down your car radio and

the 10:00 News. Turn down
the infomercials and
the bathroom fan.

If you are in Chico, in Marysville,
in the McMansions of Rocklin or parked
along the Yuba,

mute your cellphone. Quiet the dogs
and the children who aren't hungry.

Wake the snoring. Shush the fighting,
soothe the weeping and listen.

California is raining.

Raining hard and holy.

Raining schools and nursing homes, gas pumps
and sofas and neighbors who, last autumn
bought yams from ash once known
as Safeway.

California is raining.

Recall the work of weather,
how what's ascended turns
and touches down.

California is raining.

Be still and know
the sum of Paradise
beats on your roof.

NEVADA CITY FIRE, 1856

Emma Kerley

I heard it first, like a stampede
of mule deer, footsteps of desperate people
escaping something sinister.
The smoke was overwhelming, like my father
returning to the mines' deepest caverns,
constantly worried for his life.
Flames, like a lion's windblown mane, shifting
as it races towards its defenseless prey.
The heat on my face, like the blacksmith's ford
and the hot, hard hit of the hammer
on the anvil. My mother's hand, cold,
like the water of Rollins Lake freezing
overnight in the middle of winter.

9th Grade, Nevada Union High School
Grass Valley

REJUVENATION

Maya Khosla

That burned tree—it's the legacy, it's the beginning.
—Dominick DellaSala

Once we have looked away, once we have mourned
and banished all smoldering thoughts about the tribe
of blackened trees replacing the known world—
for now and another season—and the last long fingers
of smoke have been ushered out by wind, a ticking begins.
No one has seen them arriving in such numbers, but the birds
are neither lost nor passing through. They are simply linked tight
to the newborn scents of ash and rain, to the promise
of white fruits, the riches concealed by bark.

So were the ways of ancestors who began their journeys
as specks in the distance, some fifty thousand years ago.
Riding the miles of smoky gold, along a known line of hunger,
growing closer and closer. The rufous beat of instinct working
a migration upstream, against the flow of smoke, into
the source and its multiple treasures.

One new arrival looks bright with hope. He preens his dusk-
and-opal plumage. Others tap as if knocking on doors.
The answers have been provided by the ages, delicate
as genetic fibers coiled in every cell—beak and bone, muscle
and shiny eye. The living are awake to the profusion soon to follow.
They will grow with the diligence of all known colors unfurling
from the soil's chocolatey darkness, from the trees
re-greening come spring, from the blackness.

TREE GHOSTS ARE CRYING...

Seoha Kim

on their dead bodies.
Fumes from factories
and cars choke the air.
Achoo! Achoo!
Animals run away,
away fly the birds.
The water is rising,
rising to my knees.
Really?
Oh my god!
I see pools of oil,
mounds of trash,
dead fish floating
in the hot ocean.
Oh, my god, everywhere
carbon dioxide.
No flowers. What
is happening?
The clock says 2050.

3rd grade, Spreckels Elementary
San Diego County

BLACK FRIDAY

Phyllis Klein

Going up in smoke. How it would happen, flames,
sprinting like trees running marathons with the wind.
Like a heavy metal screech. Pounding on the door.
If you were sleeping maybe you didn't even wake up,

the fire faster, you no contestant in anything
other than living. In your little house with its garden
so dry, how the conflagration loves dehydration. Eating,
destroying, digesting everything. From above,

the smoke. Exhaust, exhaustion. Flashes of souls
climbing out. She with dementia, he in a wheelchair.
Others in cars, surrounded by a traffic jam of flaring
bandits, breaking in. No church or mortuary to call

when the whole town is gone. Disaster takes a trip,
we are breathing in the toxic air, the fumes of her couch,
his ashes. How we are connected. Today is a Black Friday.
Yesterday the living ate turkey, thankful for a body, a mouth

that tastes. The good and the grit. The ones with houses, the ones
without. Why do I try so hard to feel the pain? Today the scorch,
the poison, washed out of the air by rain. Today, the residue, memorials,
swindle of life and death, the ones still missing.

AFTER SUN YUM FENG

Ron Koertge

Homesick for the wealth I once possessed,
I drive through the best part of town.
Beautiful children in white stand politely
until a shadow opens their car door.
Miles away, a yellow airplane drops
fire retardant on another conflagration
Here, a wisp of smoke rises from a chimney,
perhaps someone burning a love letter.
I am such a fool, but I pull to the curb
and write this down, anyway.

RIVER SIDE, RAIN SIDE, FIRE SIDE

Robert Krut

A flare when you cough words, a disappearing act when you dance.
This rainstorm is from no cloud—the sun's exploded and sprays
    boiling water.
Yes, I am talking about you.
You whispered a secret into my ear, and I spoke a piece of paper.
I have built a tower designed to reverse lightning back to the sky.
Your eyelashes pull toward the moon.
Night's white pearl drowns the flames from your fingertips.
Danger isn't a bomb, danger is a drip.
I will build a thousand bridges, if that's what it takes.
The river is a tongue, and the tongue is of a holy beast.
Open, open your eyes, each without iris.
Your hand in my hand, your mouth in my ear.
The rain won't stop, and it won't stop burning.

SUN SETS

Kathy Kwan

A little girl is standing
outside the window.
Go back to sleep, she will
whisper in the dead of dawn.
Walk out to school, watch
them go back and forth.
See the stars before they
go away.
Watch the sun before it
sets.
You can see a black and
white fire raging
through the land.

5th grade, West Portal Elementary School
San Francisco

GLASS

Danusha Lameris

It's the small things that haunt: Oranges,
because my mother used to peel them for me,
slip the rough sections in my mouth. Luckys
because of the wayward boy who lit my first,
leaning against the railing of the pier. O Solo Mio
wafts up from the downstairs apartment.
Now it means all those summers.
Can't they just turn it off? I walk through
Queen Anne's lace in late September,
down to the cove where I used to meet
a man who was dying, that flower, now,
in my own vocabulary of loss. What doesn't,
in time, enter grief's lexicon? When I think of
our house after the fire, all I see are pools
of pink glass—once our ice cream bowls—
melted on the ruins.

ARS POETICA WITH RED RIDING HOOD

Devi Laskar

Suppose she moves to the edge of the forest,
spends her time staring into the eyes of night

from the window. Suppose she was raised to be
unafraid of hunger and loneliness, well-heeled
wolves. Suppose it's a symbolic journey, that

little girl from the red hood confronting the demon.
Suppose the moral arc of that story points back

to the paying audience waiting to be
entertained. The girl outwits the wolf and saves
the grandmother, right? Suppose the girl is charmed

by the cloak she wears, its bloody color, a bull-
fighter's flag beckoning or cheap travel-sized lipstick

from the convenience store. Suppose the distance
between the ordinary world and the dénouement
could be measured by a lie detector. Suppose

the girl is not a girl. Suppose she too is a wolf.
Suppose she is a lot older than the storyteller

pretends her to be. Then it's another Persephone
and Hades story, I suppose. We all know what
happens next, five red seeds causing the invention

of perennial winter. The wolf swallows
the grandmother whole before the girl rescues her,

right? No one ever mentions the crops burning,
how the girl in red is the match setting the world
and its old-fashioned ways alight, how it won't stop -

this burning - until trees and fields reduce to charcoal,
until the blinding smoke lifts, a new landscape is drawn.

WONDERING HOW IT ALL STARTS

Michael Ann O'Grady Leaver

I move in supplication
towards the mother of granite
with her still and creased face.
I gentle my steps
toward the twisted Bristlecone pines,
polished red and gold

I bow to the desert with her hooded eyes.
She who wears a skin of leather and spikes
sharing fierceness with badger,
tenderness with Clarkia

There is something dangerous here
waiting impatiently to be released.
The delicate fingertips of the scorpion,
curling under a flash of fire in high country,
my body attempting to speak
to inattentive clouds

SECRETS

Sophia Li

The glistening
white moon taught
me how to
sleep at night.
The golden sun
taught the world
to rise during
the bumpy dawn
The shaking
forest has secrets
to tell you:
You are strong.
Don't give up.
You can make it through.

———

5th Grade, West Portal Elementary School
San Francisco

WILDFIRE

Angelique Lopez

Breathe in my house burning.
Mi casa quemandose.
Breathe out my birthday party.
Mi fiesta de cumpleanos.
Breathe in-my friends dying.
Mis amigos muriendose.
Breathe out a new house.
Nueva casa.
Breathing in losing electricity.
Perdiendo electricidad.
Breathe out food.
Comida.
Breathe in losing your room.
Perdiendo mi cuarto.
Breathe out a new friend.
Nuevo amigo.
Breathe in no food.
No comida.
Breathe out I met my Grandpa.
Conoci a mi abuelo.
Breathe in losing your family.
Perdiendo mi famila.
Breathe out my school.
Mi escuela.

———

3rd Grade, Flowery Elementary School
Sonoma

WILDFIRE SPREAD

Denise Low

Branching powerline sparkles
detour transfer stations. Electrify
backfeed to light Santa Rosa.

Shut off of the geysers in hills
along Dry Creek Valley. Hear
dendritic chortle of generators.

Arid gullies spider slopes.
Junipers' splayed leaves repeat
ready to burst flammable pitch.

Red helicopters loop overhead
pouring water on grass tinder.
Smoke billows dust devil blades.

TIME MACHINE FIREPLACE

Bia Lowe

Yesterday my eighty-year-old brother
emailed us a jpeg of what was left.
Already a cliché in this age of burning:
the cremains of our home around a lone chimney.

The sunlight in the photo was acid yellow,
forensic bright, and the ash left an ochre tint
syphoning out the other colors,
like sepia prints of days gone by.

Referring us to the old brick fireplace, he wrote,
that was where we sang 'Downtown',
not to orient us in the wreckage,
but rather to coax us, like Rod Serling,
into another dimension, conjuring a room
where walls were paneled, and colors richly Kodachrome.

Venetian Coral was Mom's lipstick, *Indigo* Dad's Levis.
Sunflower, the jumpsuit of my brother's toddler,
who teetered against our legs
as we pressed around the player piano
and readied ourselves to belt the refrain.

And when it came, salt shaker mics in hand,
oh, how we howled! ...*Down—town!*
Our voices brimmed to the ceiling
...*where all the lights are bright!*
Into the fireplace, up through the chimney,
our hilarity sailed out into the dark, airborne
to the frogs, the foxes, the stars.
Echoing.
Galaxies.
Light years.

IT WAS 3 A.M., WINTER, AND NINE MILES FROM TRUCKEE

Suzanne Lummis

and nobody better than I to tell you about
the stillness of snow at that hour, the silence

on the surface and the snow beneath the snow,
deep, white like the black of deep space—

what then, in the 50s, we called Outer Space.
It exerted a pressure. Aliens popped out of it.

Or else, the gravity of earth reeled them into
the frames of our TVs, turning in their silver disks.

A girl in the rangy, wood shingled lodge (who no one
knew better than I) had been complaining out loud

I can't sleep!, until her parents in the other
small room called out, Then Pretend to sleep!

But even then, age 11, she felt the weight of it,
The Past, history of men, that long-running fright show

that begins at dawn and goes on after the last station
has shut down for the night, and its screen fills

with crackling, battering, unresting dots, snow.
(What's on the other side where space ends?

kids used to ask. Probably off-air snow.)
She did not imagine (she wasn't that good)

the final, ravenous melt, the calving of glaciers,
rivers swelling, seas rising, ice old and obdurate

as stone giving way as if it had held, all along,
in the nuclei of its cells, like humans, the key

to its own end. But she knew after the past
would come the sci-fi scary future, maybe aliens.

Did you think some might show up in this poem?
In the Sierra Nevada, off frozen Highway 40,

In that small hour? No. Though some whisper
they're watching as we grow more alien

to each other, and the earth. And even back then,
3 A.M., winter of '62, nothing on TV, the world over,

only the peaceful slept, and the snow—the pure, numb
and numbing stuff—

which knew nothing. Or knew but didn't care.

THE DEER

Oliver Luna

I am a deer
I see the forest
getting cut down
around me I feel
the earth getting warmer
I hear the ocean waves
getting closer and closer
to me I can
taste the dry dust blowing
in my mouth in
the summer me and
my babies are
running out of
water and dying
I fear the mountain
lions getting hungry and
going to eat me

———

4th Grade, Trillium Charter School
Humboldt County

I LIVED IN THE TIME OF GREAT FIRES

Alison Luterman

on my way home from buying breathing-masks
at the medical supply store i stop at goodwill
because it calms me to walk slowly up and down the rows
fingering rayon and cotton, silk and wool...
sky outside is white with some gray and brown mixed in
like marled yarn for a sweater no one wants to wear
i have my new air filter mask over my face
which makes me look like a frowzy, anxious
bank robber who's just stopped off
to hunt for bargains on her way to a grand heist
which is how i feel about human life here on earth today
we are pulling it out of the cashbox at gunpoint
the arctic ice shelf breaking and melting, the last polar bears,
the last tigers, last years of liveable climate
as if we were getting away with something
we won't ever get away with
once again california's burning and every thought
begins and ends with fire
it's primal, the animal need to seek shelter
though all the grass is kindling now;
kindling the trees, even the sky
seems swallowed in flame...i'd say i lived
in the time of great fires but what
time comes after this is what i want to know
and who will be around to name it

WE WILL RISE

Emily Maccario

the smell of smoke burnt my lungs
as I breathed in the night's fiery air
ribbons of grey and black smoke
billowed out around the mountains
my mind started racing
what's going on?
fire burning our precious town
no time to run back
no time to pack
stay safe, don't risk it
minutes turned into hours
hours turned into days
days into weeks
finally smoke disappears
trees burnt
houses turned to ash
families grieving
we have to have hope
because we will rise
we will rise like a phoenix
and fly over our new beginning

———

11th grade, Middletown High School
Lake County

THE VANISHING

Moira Magneson

once there was
        you sweet pika
                thick pelt & saucer ears

tiny tumble
        of energy
                scampering over

Sierra rock
        gathering grass-seed
                & forget-me-nots

when the summers
        grew too long
                & cruel you fled

to higher cooler ground
        & when the heat
                grew hotter still

you fled again
        again again
                until there was

no more fleeing
        no more mountain
                to climb

only the sky's
        blue grieving
                holding you in

its boundless gaze
        before your
                final leaving

OFFERINGS UNRECEIVED

Eileen Malone

A large distant field of stubble has been set ablaze
to hold back the wind-driven wildfire

bishops in flaming red armor with eyes so hot
they warm the hands they pass over them

hose into the gray smoke, pour oblations
into red-gold flares

a hill of dark houses leans into the heat
that feeds and quenches

night falls around the airfoils of the fire
blisters on its own breathing skin

the priests tell us a canyon fire is not sacrifice
it is about sacrifice

the ecclesiastical canons we live with,
the forfeiture, relinquishment, we die from

the evacuated fill their cars and trucks
as much as they can in their urgent haste

screech down the roads, scream up their prayers
beg for mercy, damn everything almighty

red knights retreat to the whoosh
of the slow pulse of helicopter blades

self-consumed, the blaze throws itself back
leaves all offerings unreceived.

THOUGHTS AT THE CARMELITE MONASTERY

Seretta Martin

How the Carmelite nuns
must have been shaken and prayed
for their rose-ringed green parakeets
the day fire swept up the canyon.
I miss those childhood days when nuns
who never showed their faces
spoke softly giving
holy cards through the turnstile.
I miss the chorus of their parakeets
in a hidden garden on the canyon's edge,
yet, at the front gate a gardenia scent
of vanilla and spice still lingers.
Life follows you posing
as a shepherd and religion
is based on opposites: sin and salvation,
earth and heaven, fire and ice.
There was no time to open cages,
when fire swept up the canyon
and later, gardeners found burnt eggs.

GUALALA WINTER

Kathleen McClung

Keep dreaming of gray deer asleep in woods
as sheets of rain claim every living thing—
tailor bees, bracelet cones, chipmunks, hawk broods
high up in nests that sway but last. Each wing,
leaf, stem of fern—soaked through, wet to the core—
endures these January storms we track,
evade behind our screens, our twice-locked doors.
Nervous, we curse old roofs, new leaks. Come back.
Mend quietly what's torn. Listen to wind.
Confuse it with Pacific surf close by,
cars crossing flooded roads. Gray deer may find
logs hollowed out, may curl inside, stay mostly dry
under mossed bark. Or not. Our sun will rise,
night storms will end. We animals open our eyes.

IT'S ONLY DAWN

Penelope Moffat

It's only dawn, sun blazing
through oak heart, but
it could be a closer fire
lighting veins and capillaries,
turning the sky orange.
Leaves and branches
are a latticework of sugar
waiting to be melted
in the fire's mouth.
Soon the sun will ride
high overhead,
soon the air will blue,
mirroring the lake below,
soon heat will rise without
a hint of smoke. As if
nowhere in the world
the world is burning.

BARED

Rooja Mohassessy

The small phalanx has returned, bustling over dandelions. I put off
mowing for a third morning and listen; the sunny flowers give, tousled
under one bee then another; by noon they fold up or go to seed.

I welcome the quiet in the wake of the bees—a lapse in the drone
of weed-whippers, clearing dry brush and chain saws felling bone-
stripped ponderosas. Near and far, we make the air pulsate with noise.

Back to back from dawn till two, then again at sundown, we make room,
more defensible room for fire trucks, evacuation routes. I have plenty
of visibility now—the woods a manicured park of blue oaks, silky
   madronas,

naked up to the waist, they peel before my eyes. I walk the dog, check on
toyon at the bend in the road; it came out in June—the thick
   creamy clusters
quickly wilted like a bouquet in the musty hands of an anxious bride.

Now it hangs with waxy red berries dented black as tooth decay.
  To think
Hollywood received its name from this scrub, her spot-bald boughs
gracing centerpieces at Christmas. She could poultice a wound, soften

thirst, fresh or dried then ground, she would feed me—as she did
   the Muwekma
Ohlone, the American Robin, the mockingbird—with her pomes,
   her leaves
hesitant as a rose. She leans messy and fungus-ridden over the
   scotch-broom.

I've seen them take cover here at these two brambles—the hare, transfixed
at their feet by the incoming headlight; the proud doe, too, the
   high priestess
of the woods wavers here at Toyon, the Terminus, the last remaining
   buffer

at the junction to our world. I walk back and down the driveway.
   Come nightfall,
creatures will tremble like stars without shadows, stare unblinking—
   the blackness
is now bared and leveled. I keep vigil, my home is lit up loud as
   a blunder.

PONDEROSA

Claudia Monpere

The pines, green triangles of light.
The pines, gathered at meadow's edge

Where rumors of drought have scorched the grasses.
To observe this particular light is to pray

to unexpected layers and dusty sediments.
Too long have the bones been stacked.

Longer than the birth of the first galaxy
there is that much grief.

The sky's shawl unravels.
She knits and knits and still the threads

are naked, burn boiled in the grief pot
drenched in the surveillance of stars.

THE PARTY CRASHERS OF PARADISE

Indigo Moor

We bum-rushed the stage,
      this gig in Butte County.
A hundred flaming fan dancers open
      for us, take the town like fire-
fruit dropped in hell. A blackout
      curtain tossed over the sun.

The drummer goes High Hat
      on some propane tanks.
Shit got real. Crowd squeal-
      tone deaf. Nothing croons
like charred pines.   Or
      An arpeggio of screeching hawks.

A microbus humps a Mercedes
      behind a burning bush.
      It's Paradise. These things happen.

We showcase crippled deer
chewing singed hooves.
      A scorched tabby in a bird bath.
      Knotted oaks and pine cones
            Erupting like roman candles.

Our crooner scats embers
over the middle school like rainbows,
      through the blind eye
      of the monkey bars.

      First, Burrowing Owls
bake into tender bites. Then
a grandmother. Roasted manna
hails down, picking the locks
      on a child's lungs

until the wailing of fire engines
finds its twin, before lurching
        to a dead crescendo.

After 17 days, we've torched
                EVERYTHING.

Except the Starbucks.
We own our sacred altars,
        Our angry gods of WiFi.

The Fire Marshall shuts us down.
        There's a blood cry
                in the curtain calls.
The whole damn town was screaming.
        Something like an encore.

HAIKU SONNET FOR SAN FRANCOSCO CLIMATE

Amanda Moore

All we talk about
is weather, how the fog horn
signifies summer,

And was there enough
rain or snow last winter to
plump the lakes and creeks?

And isn't it hot
inland, a heat wave across
the nation's middle.

Now we have a new
season: fire with ashfall
and dark yellow skies.

What terrible blossoms will
we harvest come spring?

GRAY TEARS

Alejandro Morales

Early one morning
I walk out to the barranca
Look out to the abandoned
Simons Brick
Company Yard #3
where I was raised

Witness a conflagration
bulldozers crush
factory buildings
and workers' houses
fires cover the 345 acres

Everything in flames
smoke streaks upward
into the deep blue
morning sky
like upside-down
gray tears

SCORCHING EMBERS

Marlowe Musser

I am fire, warming the homeless
lighting your campfires and roasting
your marshmallows spreading
ashes of friends and enemies
I illuminate your house when
the power goes off but
I also destroy your home
burning it to a crisp
I catch you on fire scorching
embers digging into your skin
I light up the trees as if
they were my matches
I search for a field of dry grass to play on
I always seem to accidently
destroy a few houses but
you cannot blame me
I am only playing just like you do
only I am dangerous
I always get confused when
fire fighters kill my children
My home is a volcano
I flicker, I blaze, I burn
I destroy but you can't
blame me because
I am fire

―――――

5th Grade, Park School
Mill Valley

WORLD WILDFIRE

Justin Nguyen

The heat
sucking up trees,
burning down
houses,
into pieces of
ash and dust.
Electric wires cracking
and exploding,
bursting and detonating
into wildfires.
Animals are suffering,
plants, too.
Wildfires are taking down
earth, getting stronger
and more furious.
I want to save the world,
create the World,
help put it back together.

4th Grade, Washington Carver Elementary
San Diego

WINTER REVISIONS

Chris Olander

Cutting back dead
  dying limbs
    enhances the form's foliage
     rewards us twice:
image lines fire cleansed.

Stack small limbs, branches:
  abstract for quail, towhee
    hawk, snake, lizard
     increase insect markets—
restore wild life diversity.

Shadow dance circles along
  fire lines between winter rains:
    fuel lessons—with smoke
     celebrate full moon rising
solstice storm clouds consuming stars.

Burn grass—scatter ash—chant—
  nourish oak, manzanita
    buck brush, wildflowers
     feed wild life—
cut up limbs for Bar-B-Que coals.

Salmon grilled slow
  in barter's marinade
    mining niche—telling tales
     landscape economics—
renewing oak-pine forest.

The way earth people work it:
  far back—beyond the historic barns
    when stacked stone rituals appeased
     fire spirit's dry wind rage—
maintain them flames—tame!

SURVIVAL SUITE

J. O'Nym

Before the wind changed direction

In the time it took us to open the door and look up,
the pitch dark sky burned a deep red, like the eye
of a black-crowned night heron. Pillars of thick smoke
shot upward, one every thirty seconds as each home
turned to ash. Devouring all, spitting fire ten stories,
Diablo set its gaze upon us. We didn't yet know
that the cars screaming down our street and wheeling
up over the sidewalk were driven by the lucky.

We have awakened to a world on fire

She draws us a map of the way out, the survival route.
She draws it from memory—starting with the memory of dying
and stepping onto the path of sheer will. She has learned every possible
way to live, has absorbed the melodies of the madrone, knows every stand
of volatile eucalyptus, steers us away from canyons and creek-beds.
We must flee the Valley of the Moon. No time to mourn the richest purple
ever imagined, madeira, alive with bees atop Bennett mountain.
She is in love, and so, knows every curve in the road, every trail,
    every rise.

Since the firestorm

We park our car facing out, tank full, go-bag in back. List on the fridge,
glow-in-the-dark tape on the handles of cases. If one trip—these four,
if two—these, too, if three—the rest. And yes, we've practiced this
    escape math:
In fourteen minutes, her Hummingbird, my Precision, her electric,
    my acoustic,
the Nord and QU-16. Boots, pants, shirt at each side of the bed.
    Headlamps, masks,
phones and keys. At night, if I think I'm too tired to put everything
    in its place,
awake, I dream a wall of flames whipping sideways, no help on the way.

Look up and to the east

Thousands of pine, now charred toothpicks, etched black ink.
Hood Mountain is bare, stands in stunned silence.
Here below, an influx of cedar waxwings and yellow-rumped
warblers punctuate the ruckus of crows. Hope surrounds us.
Just this morning, rippling beneath our boat, a beveled cumulus drifts,
white on blue, and with its twin sky above, takes another breath.

SANCTUARY AT DUSK

Sarah Pape

—written on November 8, 2019, a year after the Camp Fire

We drive through the back roads to catch
        snow geese at fly off
        watch the blue skyline unfettered
        but for the wisps of

           rice field smoke.

Their bodies gathered in the runoff,
        white and cacophonous
        as if their team scored. The crowd roars.
        Mosquitoes weave above our heads,

           herding language,

caution between us and the mirrored moon
        in the arms of waterlogged trees.
        They lift in shifts, flapping, shimmering
        feathers against an ochre

           horizon, their calls

to each other louder still, *Farewell*, we sing. *You beauties*, she says.
        In the fringe of cluttered figures, lines right
        them into more than, more than arrows,
        an errant goose goes against the pack to

           her place in the shape she knows.

It has been one year since the end of our belief in the world's survival,
        In its place, a hue of smoke and cold that crossed
        out the sun. I think, *We will never not know*
        how it ends. Next to me, she gasps again

           and again, this moment of departure.

HARDHAT PILLOW

Walter Pavlich

              I am
an outline in the ash.
Others sleep without moving,
nailed down by weariness.
Roots bum circuits beneath us.
My axe won't kill any more
shadows tonight. A fuse and wet
fingers touch in each of us.
I am too tired for water.
Tomorrow we'll find two sparrow
anatomies that did the fire-
dive off the powerlines,
fell to start this one.
They'll write the checks for next
month's bills. They'll feed
us. Their small decisions brought
us here, the coolest place
in the fire. A thunderhead
passes over, scattering us
in any direction. Mine—
a mercury drop swimming
around the palm of a hand.
No, a pearl
of rain slipping out of
the wind-tipped skillet
of a nasturtium leaf.

FIRE LINE

Connie Post

The fire starts like a bad conversation
spreading through wilderness
jumping from one tree to another

people watch from miles away
the smoke rising
like sin from a body

weeks later
the charred earth remains
like a welt on the land

eventually the soil understands
the language of submission
how to stay quiet when night comes

planes will fly overhead
noticing the edges of black
—how a loss is contained

as summer leaves
the fields seem to heal
the deepest green seeps to the surface
like old discolored blood from a bruise

everyone is quiet for a while
months pass
everyone forgets
drives by the quiet hills
as if they are redeemed

then in fall
the rain begins
continues on and on
like a story without chapters

how easily a mud slide happens
how easily a mind succumbs

and when they come to look for you
they will have to move
the granules of earth aside
with their bare and swollen hands

CALIFORNIA TRIPTYCH

Dean Rader

Cy Twombly, Lilium, Triptyque (1964)

All morning I have been thinking about catastrophe—
how many I have missed, which one will be the last,
how many I've caused, which one will be the last.
News reminds me of the line
right in the middle of the beginning and the end—
the end of what, the beginning of what,
I cannot say. All I know is off in the distance,
a bell is ringing, calling me to something
I knew was already on its way.

+

The land such as it is is always with us—

                    a memory we keep remembering.

Immanence,

        always lurking around the bar,

                is waiting for Absence to arrive.

I am waiting for the call note of Duty

            to sing me back to the shore.

I have been floating all day alone,

            the waves suddenly larger than my boat.

+

Tonight: a fist of smoke pressing into the air,
       drawing itself into a canvas of absence—
far field of erasure and eradication,
       traceries without a trace, both melt and freeze.

Below, I see typography erasing itself
       Not all maps are internal.
From here, my state, like this life,
       seems everywhere and nowhere—

OCTOBER 23, 1978

Judie Rae

We hung the front door
the day of the fire,
our remodel almost complete.

The inferno had other plans.

I grieve now
not for things lost,
but for my ignorance
in not knowing
we all needed to mourn.

With upbeat voice,
belief in the possible,
and a huge naiveté,
I told my children:
We're fine. The animals
are fine. It was just
a house.

Fifteen years later,
watching on tv
the Malibu burn
yet again,
I learned my folly.

Tears flowed down
my face as I grieved
for the first time,
our loss.

Sometimes sorrow
is a long time in coming.

SMOLDERING

Michael Riedell

Even two years on, any poem about the fires
still smells of smoke. Some words glow
with embers that haven't yet died: memory has its own desires.
Turns out everything burns, valleys and houses, cars, clothes.
Kate had just tied my tie when the text came.
No school. I went anyway and checked in with the principal
when he got the call, the word, the name
of the student I knew well, the girl we'd later lose in the hospital.

Poems are like magic baskets--you can shove into them
more than you'd ever think they could hold: her name, Kressa,
the wall of smoke I saw over Redwood Valley, the friend
who said she saw asphalt flow like black lava,
and so much more. The poem still smolders. It breathes the oxygen
we use to blow on those last coals, remembering, again and again.

TREES HAVE A LIFE SPAN — JELLYFISH LIVE FOREVER

Cindy Rinne

For Sandra Rowe

Eucalyptus bark smelled of ash. I went to the museum on the wrong day for a talk about monotypes. The firemen cooled down the melted glass of my kitchen window, I found my grandmother's jade ring and his mother's porcelain doll mixed in the embers. Only the gelatinous body of the swimming pool didn't burn. My kids used to swim three times-a-day. I weeded the herb garden and talked to our two box turtles (good listeners). One turtle survived the charring buried under damp earth. I watched men take the scorched cement, branches, twigs of my home up Golondrina Drive. People don't know how to speak to my inner bark. Three days after the fire a woman told me she wished her house would burn. Empty the clutter and build a new home. I left the discussion. No brains, bones, or heart. Root ball upside-down. Tips searching for soil. Instead, stole into the printmaking workshop. Found my artist friend perched on a stool. She quit teaching during a long illness. Medusa singing toward the immortal. In the foothills above my house, I trespassed a blackened empty lot. Single tree survived. One step at time to reclaim your voice as an artist, mother, healer. She spoke of breathing pores and sensory nerves. Understood shackles, lynching, flames. Her prints of crowns, crowns of heads, tree crowns. The short, paint-chipped wooden ladder leaned on the trunk. Creaking as I climbed the rungs, rested, and watched the city open like tentacles.

MELTED SILK

Finley Robinson

Oh, water,
you trickle and drip down the slimy smooth
rocks you splash and crash into a pool
for a bright orange fox
Oh, water,
the waves you create
are the things that keep surfers
out late
Oh, water,
you weave the mist out
over the land as waves bubble
and crash against the sand
Oh, water,
you rush all your deep blue
sadness down it wears away
and floods a tiny
little town
Oh, water, you slip through clouds'
grasp and fall you drip drip down
and splash over all
Wet, drizzle, overflow
tides, puddle, undertow

—————

5th Grade, Park School
Mill Valley

THINGS I DISCOVERED AFTER

Maria Rosales

Camp Fire, Paradise November 8th 2018

I

Clay outlasts everything else.
Porcelain nestles
intact, cushioned in ash.
Fridge, dishwasher, stove, all
the fussy rituals of daily life
vaporized. Think
about the layers of a house
walls, insulation, ceiling, heavy beamed rafters,
attic, roof, tiles... my insignificant
furniture, trinkets
condensed into three feet
of ash. Then, rain, flash flood, sludge.
My Pompeii.

II

Evacuation orders were lifted
Right around Christmas. I came up after New Year,
almost eight weeks after the fire. I dug.
It's toxic, you said. Yes
but so is not searching. There are only a few things.
One is the sapphire and diamond ring you gave me
at our twenty year mark. You joked
that you figured I was worth it by then.
Maybe not a joke. I dug
where my jewelry was hidden
in a locked cabinet in the garage.
Considering all that fell to the flames at that spot –
roof, rafters, camping gear, I expected to dig several feet.
But, after just a few inches of fine grey silt, it offered itself to me.
A congealed lump of twisted chains and beads
fused to a statue of the Madonna.

III

Madonna Gaia
You haunted the halls of the convent. I quaked in bed,
watched you walk through walls of the dormitory.
Really, I did. But I was a believer then,
or obedient.   Are they the same thing?
They stripped you
of your sex, perpetual virgin.
Despite my rejection of all that whispered of sin
somehow I took you with me. In with my sacred
totems, I placed your statue, eyes downcast,
chaste robe unruffled by the babe on your hip.

How is it that you sealed yourself
to my treasure?
Welded deep in that rock of chain and beads
may be the 20 year sapphire ring.
I will not chip away to find it.
It may be there.
Like so many things that matter,
that may be enough.
Madonna,
I, who am letting go
beg you
to hold on.

FIRE SKY

Lisa Rosenberg

First   sweet smoke

       grass-heads and deadwood

the undergrowth

       undone in one

swath of heat

       how

faultless

       the motes

     the dull

lens of dusk

all day

     mantle of ash

umber streams

      untold

inscrutable

   beginnings

COMMUNION

Kim Scheiblauer

Santa Rosa 2017

We inhale—
one hundred miles away—

cells of your asphalt drive,
atoms of car paint
and melted tire,

molecules from scalding oils—
eucalyptus, valley oak,

the particulates
of burned vineyards.

Blown to us—
patina of doorknobs
and locks, burnished keys,

curled photos,
household bills, flash drives—
now vapor.

Taste residue of ash
from combustible collars,
cotton or silk,
laces like wicks;

we receive
the now invisible,

vanished fingerprints,
so many last breaths,
whatever is left light enough
to rise like smoke.

We breathe it all in,
cannot cough it out.

This is when we kneel,
or should,
char on our tongues.

"IF" TURNS TO "WHEN"

John Schneider

I.
Driving through Gary Indiana, it's late August,
the birthplace of the Jackson Five and U.S. Steel,
men in sleeveless undershirts over rolled–up
jeans and Red Wing boots
sweat like Brando in "A Streetcar Named Desire."
They smoke on street corners, wait for something to happen.

And then snow begins to fall!
And that confuses me
this heavenly offering in the wrong season.
I turn the wipers on, sickened when I recognize
these swan-white snowflakes for what they are:
lead and benzene particulate matter
emitted from steel mill stacks.
One of the men starts dancing
with what by now I see as sarcastic resignation.

II.
Years later, on a mid-summer night
we awaken. Coughing. Choking.
"What we fear most, we call impossible, turn it into 'if'."
   Wildfire Preparedness: purchase N95 respirators
The bedroom wallpapered
in thick bluish gray smoke and fear.
Inhaling, we wheeze and gasp,
   keep an air purifier in a safe room,
exhaling, our breath hangs in the air
with the stench of burnt shower curtains and mattress foam
forming images of death's
shadow against once-bright walls.

Driven away from the safety of home
   keep 100 foot hoses on each side of the house

cars crawling behind cars crawling
like beetles that have lost their wings.
The white stuff falling: the opposite of manna.

    rake needles and leaves, clear brush near house
Dreamers awakened by a fear no longer private.
Flocks of usually solitary geese and ducks huddle together
on the pond, surprised-confused
    create defensible space, screen under deck areas
I think they must be terrified too.
    keep a go bag, have a plan
"The ultimate fear being we will lose everything."
I can feel the warmth of the undertaker's hands.
"We take stock of all that we have,
not yet ready to let go."

III.
I had become immune
to smoky air and skies darkened from wildfires
    close doors and windows, light on in every room
routine as the change of seasons.
"We do all the right things to stay out of harm's way"
    get out when told to leave
"What we prepare for will surely happen!"
"It is only a wildfire in Yosemite
200 miles away,
we have nothing to worry about,"
death's hounds kept on a leash this time.
    leave a sign in window "evacuated."

ALWAYS FIRE SEASON

Kim Shuck

Flame reads the stories of tree rings out loud and for the last time

Thursday our kitchen fire alarms went off
Breathing lives as we were
Breathing the collected things
Of lives
The fur and claws
The feathers
The ID cards and photographs and pocket lint

Here in the bay our sunrises and sunsets have changed

Extreme wildfires
Part of the new normal weather
An always fire season
We know the forests by when they burned
Whose ashes on our windshield?
Whose ashes in our skin
In our lungs?

The cars, immobile, fused into the melted roadway

Less rain
Cracked lips of hillside
Flaking skin of
Flood plain
And the dice roll of pet sparks
Conditionally captured in wire
Running the dry west

Curled and silvered fingers of pine as monument

FAKE

Aurora Smith

The glowing eyes only seeing green
no, not the green of trees
It's the green of greed
filling our minds with envy
Envy of the oblivious
who stand on a golden pedestal
the ones who only see green
they look down us
The creative ones
that watch and protest
as we see the world
as it's turning grey
Watching from a desert
that once was a great lake
The writers held underwater
The artists gone
As the oblivious strip away the life
strip away the originality
from upon a pedestal
as we are underwater
Held under florescent lights
everything in a lab
to control us
Take away the color
Take away the air
Make us forget the smell
of fresh pine
running through the air
not the car fresheners
the take away the blue
of the sea
and the powder white
of the arctic
Take away the sweet taste of strawberries
or the tangy between
green apples compared to purple

Watch as it burns
replacing our minds with cotton candy
that dissolves with new information
Take a minute to breathe clean air, not smog
the song of the wind, not a freeway
taste a cherry, not the sugar candy named for it
paint the world
Please realize we can still
roam free

11th Grade, Pacific Community Charter High School
Mendocino County

AN OFFERING

SA Smythe

Stop me if you've heard this one before
So that I can tell it again, and savor it.
I am here, yet they think of me as a relic.
Not forgotten, but unglorified
A rough beast with a hashtagged accent of defeat,
A weak heart, and a Bethlehem slouch.

I often find myself both sought after and shunned—
Unable to speak my own name if I wanted—eternally emptied,
Made to mourn the loss of any meaning I might yet make
Like a silenced clap of thunder, technicolor turned to ashes.
It seems that so many I've loved have wanted me dead,
Ground down into the ancestral mosaic of past and present gods.

Earthly siblings, sweet apparitions: can we sanctify ourselves into
    new life?
I cannot warn the others of the coming storm alone,
Cannot take shelter from storms already here, and look! Just look.
Everywhere blood clings to the leaves, soot gnaws at the lungs
There's no water for miles, and soon all you can say is:
Well, we should've listened for the thunder.

Still, I was not the first to dream another world,
To crave the teeming darkness of the ocean floor,
Stories I would never fully know. With this I exalt myself,
Shapeshift into my harbinger skin. We have always been on the move.
Lithe and wild and dangerous, we grow new lungs,
Spread our palms across the dirt and tend to new leaves.

But I can never forget the body that came before.
Acidic grief dries out along the cracks in this new flesh,
Phantom bruises from when them did hush up the clap, thief the color.
I divine myself as Ochumaré, a messenger with an offering
That you may call me rainbow serpent,
Sibling, lover, or freedom traveler

That in case language doesn't express desire, but hides it,
You must remember to reach only for the neither thing,
To be righteously unashamed of this grief until the otherwise comes
Until that time when we may name ourselves whole, if not holy,
And stop eulogizing the project of living long enough to see
That it has yet to come, and so can never die.

CONTROL BURN

Gary Snyder

What the Indians
here
used to do, was,
to burn out the brush every year
in the woods, up the gorges,
keeping the oak and the pine stands
tall and clear
with grasses
and kitkitdizze under them,
never enough fuel there
that a fire could crown.

Now, manzanita,
(a fine bush in its right)
crowds up under the new trees
mixed up with logging slash
and a fire can wipe out all.

Fire is an old story.
I would like,
with a sense of helpful order,
with respect for laws
of nature,
to help my land
with a burn, a hot clean
burn.
       (manzanita seeds will only open
       after a fire passes over
       or once passed through a bear)

And then
it would be more
like,
when it belonged to the Indians

Before.

ANXIETY

Alan Soldofsky

You feel the friction on the front porch
when the wind switches around to the north.
 Jets roaring overhead, taking off the
wrong way. It's the start of fire season.
The tanoaks and eucalyptus have dried
out. The air is sinking, gusting over
the ridgetops. At dusk a sallow half-moon
ascends through the branches like something coughed up.
There's a red flag warning. If it won't
cool down, they'll cut the power off
because all this brush might go up in flames
like last year when the high-tension lines exploded,
and a whole town nearly burnt to nothing.
There's a faint scent of skunk in the gutter,
the pavement overcooked. How will you live
without AC or refrigeration?
The food will spoil, and you'll sweat through your sheets.
You can't stop yourself from twitching all night
in your bed huffing the darkness.
An orange aura glowers above the hills,
where you suspect the birds have gone,
a flock of swallows twittering in
the distant skies. Once in a while you find
one of their scorched, electric bodies laying
on the ground, a bit of feathered putty
half buried under a mound of ashes
which you carefully step around, not to
touch it with your hot and swollen foot.

PROXIMA CENTAURI, OR ANNIVERSARY OF THE FIRE

Wren Tuatha

Tell me what you know about dismemberment.
—Bhanu Kapil

•

its literalness, the resistance of the dead bay branch through loppers into my wrist and elbow, mutual rigidity, what the tree and I saw of consuming flame that morning, the bone and crack and hunt of it

•

its joining, my fulcrum on the tool, arthritis in fingers and shoots, our fibers under skins, container/identity. acceptance, the tree and me of it, absorbing the sun on a November day that shouldn't be this warm

•

the way the virus of weather is personal and really not, hiker and boot to ants carrying food. the virus of weather leaves us defined as survivors, watchful, while processing our dead branches

•

the stupid green of it, leafing a young bay salad at the trunk, the dna of persistence without a basis, the red berry clueless-ness, one single offering, held forward on a new growth green hand. a deer or bear might carry its seeds to the next canyon so

I will tell you what I know about fire. it meets you where you burn, says, do over, do differently, remember that you're an animal. it knows you, spark on a fingertip across a cat's back or Proxima Centauri keeping its gravitational distance. my dis-memberment from a green safe home is so much code in the stir of Earth and her metoo rages

•

there's a theory—we plants and animals are just vehicles, time
machines to carry our dna forward so

stupid me for composing little poems instead of stepping down
from world dominance in disgrace

NO ONE SAID IT WOULD BE EASY

Alison Turner

Horses standing blindfolded in the surf
dog sprinting into traffic
at the bottom of a dry swimming pool,
a man wrapped
in a wet sheet, an operator's voice saying
don't hang up

TV/Autumn/Fire: the smell of air burned through
the peculiar hush ash shares with snow

Cedar   Witch Creek   Marble Cone   Sand

The one seed pried open by heat

The one hour or day of pure consequence

What would you save to prove you had a life?

IT DOESN'T AFFECT YOU

Mylie Turney

It doesn't affect you, right
the changing climate
the melting ice mothers
It won't reach you, right?
the spirit of lava as
it burns through soles of others
you won't drown, right?
when the ocean claims
a new home
It definitely won't be you,
the survivor left all alone
Because you'll be dead, right?
you'll be long gone by then
but it's happening now
indiscriminatory against men
consider change
you've done it before
It will help your friends, neighbors,
family, strangers
and maybe even more

———

12th grade, Middletown High School
Lake County

CALIFORNIA'S NATURE POLLUTIONS

Osiris Valdez

N-Nature is in trouble.

A-Acid effects animals.

T-Toxic Pollutions are monsters

U-Underwater animals are being killed by plastic GHOSTS

R-Recycling plastic is better.

E-Embers are poison to nature.

P-Poison greenhouse gases, YUCK!

O-Oil slick is bad for fish and turtles.

L-Lead the way, Mother Nature!

L-Let the world be healed.

U-Underwater and ground animals stay free.

T-Transport trash to another world.

I-I love this world, don't you?

O-Oceans and rainforests stay safe.

N-Now, let's stay longer and clean this planet!

S-San Diego, let's save our EARTH!!!

———

4th Grade, Washington Carver Elementary
San Diego

SEAL RESCUE

Josefine Van De Moere

I've been swimming in the deep ocean,
water pressure against me.
I swim towards the light, but
I feel something tugging on me.

I look down and see
a plastic strap stuck on my fin.
With my mouth I try to pull it off
but it's too tight.

I've been swimming in circles
with only three fins.
I'm so hungry but I can't stop now.
I won't give up.

In the surf I see feet coming. Tan hands
reach for me. I'm afraid but I can't swim away.
The hands gently pull the plastic from my fin.
Finally, I'm free!

3rd grade, Spreckels Elementary School
San Diego County

A LETTER FROM FIRE

Ali Vandra

Sorry.
I came out of nowhere
and destroyed everything.
Like a typhoon against a stick house.
I was just hungry.
My hunger cannot be tamed though.
It's like the Yuba River in winter, rushing
and rising over land.
Sweeping away anything in its wake.
I want to be friends,
but everything I touch turns to ash.
I tried to warn you
as my hunger ran wild.
My bright red and orange lit up the sky
like a warning siren going off.
But still, I was too quick.
No warning could ever prepare you
for my destruction.
The wind tried to knock me down
and the lakes and rivers tried
to surround me.
But they did not avail.
My hunger dismisses them as a slight annoyance
in the whole scheme of things,
and ravages your home,
your family.
Sorry I cannot do anything but watch.
As if I were a fawn witnessing her mother
hit by a car. Unable to stop it.
Unable to move.
Sorry.

———

9th Grade, Nevada Union High School
Grass Valley

AFTER

Gillian Wegener

Even the black metal shelves
our father lugged from garage
to garage all those years,
even those gave way in that fury, sagged
and buckled, folded in on themselves,
the items stored there unrecognizable,
little mounds of ash,
little curls of what was
and now isn't.

•

A friend says the biggest difference
is the light, how much there is now
that the tree canopy is gone,
blackened trunks so gaunt
they barely cast shadows.

•

Somehow my brother's lot is cleared early on.
The crumpled garage doors gone.
The melted washer gone.
The skeleton of gazebo
scraped away with the ash
that was the kitchen table where
he'd left a cup of coffee
half full that last morning, gone.

•

Somehow our parents' old house survives
unscathed. A fluke.
Next door, a man, shirtless, pokes
through the ashes of his house
with what was once a ski.

•

Happy Garden Chinese is gone.
The pizza place is gone.
Safeway is gone.
Eleven churches, gone.
Ace Hardware, gone.
That little diner Dad loved, gone.

•

My friend recites the names
of streets where people died.
Don't go there, she says.
You don't want to go there.

•

At Sam's Liquors, the roof caved in
and bottles melted on their shelves.
mound of blue, mound of green,
mound of diamond-bright white,
all reflecting back daylight,
stained glass, almost sacred.

BEAUTIFUL BUT DEADLY

Liam West

Beautiful, hot, deadly, bright.
He destroys everything we know and love, fire.
Flames ripping through trees, houses, roads, anything in his
  path.
Flames can help us in many ways but
He can also destroy like a bomb.
Fire

The animals running out of the woods.
Firefighters fighting against the flames.
People's homes burned.
Forests to ashes in seconds.
Fire

Fire he's like a spiky spear elegant but deadly.
He looks beautiful but behind all the red, orange
and yellow he's evil.
He destroys not creates.
Fire

He takes everything and leaves nothing behind.
Taking toys from children.
Stealing bark from trees.
Leaving nothing in return.
Fire

The flames have past
Trees to ashes.
Houses burned to the ground.
Even though the flames have destroyed everything,
There is still hope for the smallest seed to sprout.

4th Grade, Lu Sutton Elementary School
Novato

SMOKE

Emmanuel Williams

There were gas masks in the kitchen cupboard.
There was a long narrow building by the school playground
—thick walls, no windows
for when the German bombers came.
There was always danger.
Searchlights, air-raid sirens
explosions trembling the house
always news of bad things happening.
Some nights I smelt and saw London burning
twenty miles away.
It was many years after D-day
before the nightmares faded.

Now I'm up here in the Sierra
4000 feet above the rising seas.
Drought mountain country.
Millions of dead trees, stripped of twigs and needles
standing on hot steep slopes.
Parched grass, dry brown undergrowth.
On the fridge door there's a list
things to load into the car if there's a fire
laptops, cat box, clothes, bottled water
narrow winding roads we hope will lead to safety.
Last week I was smelling smoke
remembered London burning
wished there could be another D-Day.

NEVADA CITY FIRE OF 1856

Olivia Willoughby

I saw the cloud of black smoke
crawling over Nevada City like a black cat
sneaking up on a sparrow.
The screams like screeching mine cart brakes
trying to stop, but failing.
The smell of burning wood drifted
over the town, like the rolling waters
of the Yuba. I tasted the ashes as they fell
in my mouth, like bitter snow drifting.
I turned around, the fire
was nipping at my ankles
like a dog biting at a cow's hooves.
It raced around my skirt
brushing against my legs
like Mountain Misery on a windy summer day.
The scorching heat blistered
my skin, popping like bubbles
on the rapids of the Yuba.
I tried to run away, but the flames
caught my skin. I closed my eyes
to let the pain wash over me
like sinking under water, watching
the waves move over me.

9th Grade, Nevada Union High School
Grass Valley

AND BECAUSE THEY SLEPT IN, MY FRIENDS—

Lenore Wilson

        artists, musicians, old boys
with instruments whittled from boughs
      (colors dusky not smooth but gnarled and warped)

redwood, boxwood, maple inscribed   they sleep in,

they slumber, they do,
naturally as animals—foxes chipmunks squirrels—burrowing in,
deep down (away from their toils)

        under wings of conifers, not far from brooks, little rivulets
womb like they do
hibernate   in this place, home, name it
           Paradise (their personal Elysium Valhalla, Avalon)

      you see my neighbor says, with that child-lost look on his face
in the library parking lot, with morning departing

you see, he says, about the fires,
(his eyes asquint)

they were artists, musicians, retired,
      like me, and though I've moved two hours away…

they were artists, musicians, retired, like me

I tried phoning them, you know
    and the smoke, it's so hard to breathe even here
about two hours south

and the not

      the not knowing, and

how the golden-red leaves, swirl, spin, counter-dance
(legions of them) and the not knowing

how to wrap one's head around how

do you, how they
            may not have

gotten out, or maybe tried, hunched over steering

wheels round
the image, (fixed countenance) imagine   with or without

wives, animals, instruments, their

      eyes set on the horizon as if a miracle
as if a certainly

A certainty, oh imagine them blinded by fire
(the hum of the flames which bee-hives make)

carrying their instruments
      shielded there, tucked angel like

            between elbow and waist, cradled
fiddle   mandolin   oboe (smitting there)

and just made guitar in its canvas case stretched out across
   a lap, pieta-like;
                  oh imagine and driving out, they were , or they are

sacred now, all of them, imagine.....sublime.

EYE TO EYE THEY SOLEMNLY CONVENE
TO MAKE THE SCENE

Maw Shein Win

The version, the real one,
The empire,
Azusa, Covina, Fontana.

Dialing in the 909 in blind time,
The only one left of her and his kind,
The drive-by, the skip and the skipper.

Mini-skirt mirage and dust bunnies,
Tassels and bonnets, trump card,
Wind winding round, sounding off board.

Out. Snap out of it. On the back of a flatbed.
A reappearing and disappearing
and tearing of the hair.

Clumps of sad lands and badlands
and ballads and frat beds.
Welcome to Costco, I Love You.

A burning and yearning, ballast and binge.
Stone. Dirt. Ice. White fire.
Blood dust. Stock lust. Lapdogs. Silicone and eyelets.

Teleprompters and dustbowls.
Orange groves and smokestacks.
Check the oil. Piles of soil. Spoil Him. Her. Me.

More. Tracking the score.
It's keepin' track of the fact watching them watching back.
Come come now. How. Snap. Out. Of. It. Now.

MY OLD HOUSE

Markus Wright

Come through the dark lane of cold air
like a ghost flowing through your bones.
Look around at the huge tree looking down on you.
Listen carefully for the sound of sobbing.
Walk down the block until you see a park.
Run up to the park to see if it's broken.
Smell the rain falling in the midnight sky.
Touch the rust on the monkey bars.
You can make out a human figure of a boy.
The boy is sitting on
what used to be a crimson swing.
Looking at a house 10 feet away from the park,
hear the sobbing again but it sounds close.
You can see the boy crying by the shining tears falling down.
And that boy misses his old house.
And that boy is me.

6th grade, James Monroe Elementary School
Sonoma County

BURN AFTER READING

George Yatchisin

So it seems fire can be a sort of time travel,
what when wind-whipped it can clip
an acre-a-second, something similar
to 150 cars parked in a square and each
with a hungry spark tonguing its gas tank.
Of course it's hard to say whether nothing
equals past, present, or future, as if smoke
signified something as simple as nostalgia,
a quick if sloppy kiss, the hope for romance,
for fire reminds us anything can happen
before anything does. They tell us at night
the ridge of flames will appear closer
than it really is. They tell us the wind rides
in hell's driver seat, that something with a name
seductive, with a name like a train—sundowner—
may make a blaze roll in with a tsunami of spark.
They tell us we could drown in this air, so teach
lessons of particulates, the important algebra
of the numbering of masks. Sure enough everyone
who dares to walk about does so dressed as if
for robbery or surgery, and indeed something
is stolen, something needs so much to heal.

THE FLOW

Chryss Yost

When the water comes, it brings the mountain
and sings the story of the shifting ridge,
summons green to bloom along its edge.
Shapes the hills with patient excavation.

Water comes and carries what we were:
wind-torn leaves, the old path washed away,
the swallowed reflections of hunter and prey.
Brings ash and remains of the bear flag bear.

When water comes, thirst rises for reunion
with the river. All are sullied by the journey.
What blessing to reclaim our purity,
leave the salty stories for the ocean.

We are renewed, to wonder which came first:
that flow of water or this endless thirst?

[UNTITLED]

Gary Young

The fire spared our house, turned toward the winery, and bolted down the canyon. Everyone assumed the grapes on the ridge were a loss, but when I open a bottle of Pinot from the vineyard here on Battle Mountain, 2009, the year of the blaze, the scent of ash is on the cork, and I taste the true terroir of home: sun and rain, minerality from the granite soil, and catastrophe. In this vintage, there's dark chocolate and briar in the glass, strawberry and plum in the mouth, and in the finish—smoke.

EMBER OF THE SUN

Aislyn Yuen

I am the basket made of
bear grass in the Northern Lights.
I am the bowl made of
spruce roots at night.
I am the orange fire
that burns
through the
maple forest.
I am the forest of tricks.
I am the beads made
of the embers of the sun.

3rd Grade, Francis Scott Key Elementary School
San Francisco

SONOMA COUNTY PRESTISSIMO

Mary Zeppa

October 2017

Wildfire: hills, orchards, neighborhoods.
"10 minutes. Our block was gone."

Cars melting, tires exploding.
Dogs, horses, goats on their own.

Which way does the wind howl
this morning? Is my sister's

house in Santa Rosa still safe?
And The Fountaingrove Inn,

home-away-from-home, where we
drank a Good Night Kiss

in the bar before
we laid our heads down?
*
All week on Facebook,
her family's marked SAFE.

Their van's packed, they're
ready to evacuate:

camping gear, important
papers, one album

of photos, one box
of Christmas

ornaments made
when their grown son

and daughter were small.
"In case, we have to

start over," she says
adjusting her particle mask.

CONTRIBUTORS

Kim Addonizio's most recent book is *Mortal Trash*. She lives in Oakland.

Opal Palmer Adisa's most recent book is *Love's Promise*. She lives in Oakland.

David Alpaugh's most recent book is *Heavy Lifting*. He lives in Pleasant Hill.

Lisa Alvarez's latest book is *Orange County: A Literary Field Guide*. She lives in Modjeska Canyon.

Cynthia Anderson's most recent book is *Route*. She lives in the Mojave Desert.

Daniel Ari is the Poet Laureate of Richmond.

Quinn Arthur is a third grader at Francis Scott Key Elementary School, San Francisco.

Lea Aschkenas is the author of *Es Cuba*. She lives in Fairfax.

Darvin Atkeson (cover photographer) is an American veteran and landscape photographer living in Bass Lake.

Claire J. Baker is the author of eight books including *Dear Mother*. She lives in Pinole.

Devreaux Baker's most recent book is *Hungry Ghosts*. She lives in Mendocino.

Sebastian Baker is a fifth grader at Arcata Elementary School in Humboldt County.

Joan Baranow's most recent book is *In The Next Life*. She lives in Mill Valley.

Ellen Bass's most recent book is *Indigo*. She's the former Poet Laureate of Santa Cruz, where she lives.

Ruth Bavetta's most recent book is *No Longer at This Address*. She lives in San Clemente.

Judy Bebelaar's most recent book is *And Then They Were Gone: Teenagers of Peoples Temple from High School to Jonestown*. She lives in Berkeley.

Mouad Belkhalfia is a fourth grader at Cleveland Elementary School, Oakland.

Henri Bensussen's most recent book is *Earning Colors*. She lives in Santa Rosa.

Stella Beratlis is the Poet Laureate of Modesto. Her most recent book is *Alkali Sink*.

Gene Berson's most recent book is *Raveling Travel*. He lives in Grass Valley.

Claire Blotter's most recent book is *Moment in the Moment House*. She lives in San Rafael.

Laure-Anne Bosselaar's most recent book is *These Many Rooms*. She is the Poet Laureate of Santa Barbara.

Heather Bourbeau is a member of the Writer's Grotto and lives in Berkeley.

Judy Brackett's most recent book is *Flat Water*. She lives in Nevada City.

Katy Brown lives in Davis.

Susan Browne's most recent book is *Just Living*. She (just) lives in the East Bay.

Kirsten Casey's most recent book is *Ex Vivo: Out of the Living Body*. She lives in Grass Valley.

Aileen Cassinetto is the Poet Laureate of San Mateo County.

Marcelo Hernandez Castillo's most recent book is *Children of the Land*. He lives in Marysville.

Brandon Cesmat's latest book is *Light in All Directions*. He lives in Valley Center.

Teresa Mei Chuc's most recent book is *Invisible Light*. She's the Poet Laureate of Altadena.

Susan Cohen's most recent book is *A Different Wakeful Animal*. She lives in Berkeley.

Jessica Cohn lives in Aptos.

Brad Crenshaw's forthcoming book is *A Raft of Islands*. He lives in Santa Cruz.

James Cruz is an 11th grader at Pacific High School in Ventura.

Doc Dachtler's most recent book is *Why Am I Telling You This?* He lives in Nevada City.

Amy Elizabeth Davis lives on Tongva land/in Los Angeles.

M.J. Donovan lives in Santa Cruz.

Linda Dove's most recent book is *Fearn*. She lives in the foothills east of Los Angeles.

Kim Dower's most recent book is *Sunbathing on Tyrone Power's Grave*. She's the former Poet Laureate of West Hollywood.

Cheryl Dumesnil's most recent book is *Showtime at the Ministry of Lost Causes*. She lives in Walnut Creek.

Kate Dwyer's forthcoming chapbook is *33 by 3*. She lives in Grass Valley.

Johanna Ely is the former Poet Laureate of Benicia.

Gail Entrekin's most recent book is *The Art of Healing*. She lives in Orinda.

Molly Fisk's most recent book is *Naming Your Teeth: Even More Observations from a Working Poet*. She was the inaugural Poet Laureate of Nevada County, where she lives on Nisenan land.

Mary Fitzpatrick lives in Pasadena.

Casey FitzSimons's most recent book is *More Than I Can Stand to Know*. She lives in Redwood City.

CB Follett was the inaugural Poet Laureate of Marin County. She lives in Sausalito.

Rebecca Foust's most recent book is *The Unexploded Ordnance Bin*. She lives in Kentfield and was Poet Laureate of Marin County.

Leonardo Fusaro is a tenth grader at Pacific Community Charter High School in Mendocino.

Mary Gast lives in Benicia.

Rafael Jesus Gonzalez is the Poet Laureate of Berkeley, where he lives.

Taylor Graham was the inaugural Poet Laureate of El Dorado County and lives in Placerville.

Octogenarian **Cleo Griffith** has won Second Place, California Federation of Chaparral Poets, and lives in Salida.

Group Poem is by the fifth graders of Hidden Valley Elementary School, Santa Rosa. The Poet-Teacher is Margo Perin.

Junior Gutierrez is a fifth grader at Selma Herndon Elementary in Livingston.

Lara Gularte's most recent book is *Kissing the Bee*. She lives in Diamond Springs.

Lynn M. Hansen's most recent book is *Flicker*. She lives in Modesto.

Katherine Harar is a former Statewide Director of California Poets in the Schools. She lives in San Rafael.

Cynthia Haven's forthcoming book is *The Spirit of the Place: Czeslaw Milosz in California*. She lives in Stanford.

Willow Hein is a flower farmer in Nevada County. *www.soilsisters.org*

Juan Felipe Herrera has been the Poet Laureate of California and also of the nation.

Lee Herrick's most recent book is *Scar and Flower*. He lives in Fresno.

Donna Hilbert's most recent book is *Gravity: New and Selected Poems*. She lives in Long Beach.

Brenda Hillman's most recent book is *Extra Hidden Life, Among the Days*, which won the Northern California Book Award. She lives in Kensington.

Jane Hirshfield's most recent book is *Ledger*, from Knopf Doubleday. She lives in Mill Valley.

Henry Hoffman is a fourth-grader at Lu Sutton Elementary, Novato.

Jackleen Holton's most recent book is *Devil Music*. She lives in San Diego.

Twyla Hoshida is a fourth-grader at Cleveland Elementary School in Oakland.

Jodi Hottel's most recent book is *Out of the Ashes*. She lives in Santa Rosa.

Michael Hughes is a fourth-grader at Lu Sutton Elementary School, Novato.

Maureen Hurley is a poet-teacher for California Poets in the Schools and lives in West Marin.

James Lee Jobe is the fourth Poet Laureate of Davis, where he lives.

Leeloo Johansen is a fourth-grader at Cleveland Elementary School in Oakland.

Tim Kahl's most recent book is *The Century of Travel*. He lives in Elk Grove.

Maxima Kahn's forthcoming book is *Fierce Aria*. She lives in Nevada City.

Susan Kelly-DeWitt's most recent book is *The Fortunate Islands*. She lives in Sacramento.

Terri Kent-Enborg teaches at American River College and lives in Auburn.

Emma Kerley is a ninth-grader at Nevada Union High School, Grass Valley.

Maya Khosla is the Poet Laureate of Sonoma County where she lives.

Seoha Kim is a third-grader at Spreckels Elementary School in San Diego.

Phyllis Klein's forthcoming book is *The Full Moon Herald*. She lives in Palo Alto.

Ron Koertge is the Poet Laureate of South Pasadena, where he lives.

Robert Krut's most recent book is *The Now Dark Sky, Setting Us All on Fire*. He lives in Burbank.

Kathy Kwan is a fifth-grader at West Portal Elementary School in San Francisco.

Danusha Lameris is the Poet Laureate of Santa Cruz, where she lives.

Devi Laskar's most recent book is *The Atlas of Reds and Blues*. She lives in Los Altos.

Michael Ann O'Grady Leaver lives in Berkeley.

Sophia Li is a fifth-grader at West Portal Elementary School, San Francisco.

Angelique Lopez is a third-grader at Flowery Elementary School, Sonoma.

Denise Low is a former Poet Laureate of the state of Kansas and lives in Healdsburg.

Bia Lowe resides in San Francisco.

Suzanne Lummis's most recent book is *Open 24 Hours*. She lives in Los Angeles.

Oliver Luna is a fourth-grader at Trillium Charter School, Humboldt County.

Alison Luterman's most recent book is *Desire Zoo*. She lives in Oakland.

Emily Maccario is an eleventh-grader at Middletown High School, Lake County.

Moira Magneson's most recent book is *He Drank Because*. She lives in Placerville.

Eileen Malone was unofficially named the Poet Laureate of Broadmoor Village, where she lives.

Seretta Martin's forthcoming book is *Overtaking Glass*. She lives in Santee.

Kathleen McClung's forthcoming book is *Temporary Kin*. She lives in San Francisco.

Penelope Moffat lives in Culver City.

Rooja Mohassessy was born in Iran but now lives in Dobbins.

Claudia Monpere teaches at Santa Clara University and lives in Oakland.

Indigo Moor's forthcoming book is *Everybody's Jonesin' for Something*. He is the Poet Laureate of Sacramento.

Amanda Moore teaches at The Urban School of San Francisco and surfs on Ocean Beach.

Alejandro Morales's most recent book is *River of Angels*. He lives in Santa Ana.

Marlowe Musser is a fifth-grader at Park School in Mill Valley.

Justin Nguyen is a fourth-grader at Washington Carver Elementary School, San Diego.

Chris Olander teaches with California Poets in the Schools and lives in Nevada City.

J. O'Nym lives in Santa Rosa.

Sarah Pape's most recent book is *Ruination Atlas*. She lives in Chico.

Walter Pavlich, 1955-2002, author of *Sensational Nightingales*, lived in Davis.

Luis Antonio Pichardo (translator)'s most recent book is *Love Notes*. He lives in Los Angeles.

Connie Post's new book is *Prime Meridian*. She lives in Livermore.

Dean Rader's most recent book is *Self-Portrait as Wikipedia Entry*. He lives in San Francisco.

Judie Rae's most recent book is *The Haunting of Walter Rabinowitz*. She lives in Nevada City.

Michael Riedell's most recent book is *Small Talk & Long Silences*. He lives in Ukiah.

Cindy Rinne's latest solo book is *Moon of Many Petals*. She lives in San Bernardino.

Finlay Robinson is a fifth-grader at Park School, Mill Valley.

Maria Rosales's most recent book is *Time to Fly*. She lives in San Ysidro and Baja.

Lisa Rosenberg's most recent book is *A Different Physics*. She lives in Menlo Park.

Kim Scheiblauer lives in Soquel.

John Schneider lives in Berkeley.

Kim Shuck is the Poet Laureate of San Francisco.

Aurora Smith is an eleventh-grader at Pacific Community Charter High School, Mendocino.

SA Smythe's forthcoming books are *proclivity* and *Where Blackness Meets the Sea: On Crisis, Culture, and the Black Mediterranean*. They live in the Los Angeles basin on Tongva land.

Gary Snyder's most recent book is *The Great Clod: Notes and Memories on the Natural History of China and Japan*. Described as the "Poet Laureate of Deep Ecology," he lives on the San Juan Ridge.

Alan Soldofsky's most recent book is *In the Buddha Factory*. He lives in San Jose.

Wren Tuatha's most recent book is *Thistle and Brilliant*. She lives in Magalia.

Alison Turner's most recent book is *What to Do in an Emergency*. She lives in Los Angeles.

Mylie Turney is a twelfth-grader at Middletown High School, Lake County.

Osiris Valdez is a fourth-grader at Washington Carver Elementary School, San Diego.

Josefine Van De Moere is a third-grader at Spreckels Elementary School, San Diego.

Ali Vandra is a ninth-grader at Nevada Union High School, Grass Valley.

Gillian Wegener's most recent book is *This Sweet Haphazard*. She lives in Modesto.

Liam West is a fourth-grader at Lu Sutton Elementary School, Novato.

Emmanual Williams's most recent book is *An Old Dog Dreaming*. He lives in Miramonte.

Olivia Willoughby is a ninth-grader at Nevada Union High School, Grass Valley.

Lenore Wilson was the Poet Laureate of Napa Valley, where she lives.

Maw Shein Win is the Poet Laureate of El Cerrito, where she lives.

Markus Wright is a sixth-grader at James Monroe Elementary School, Sonoma.

George Yatchisin's most recent book is *The First Night We Thought the World Would End*. He lives in Santa Barbara.

Chryss Yost is a former Poet Laureate of Santa Barbara, where she lives.

Gary Young was the inaugural Poet Laureate of Santa Cruz, where he lives.

Aislyn Yuen is a third-grader at Francis Scott Key Elementary School, San Francisco.

Mary Zeppa's most recent book is *My Body Tells Its Own Story*. She lives in Sacramento.

CREDITS / PERMISSIONS

"Let Them Not Say," by Jane Hirshfield, was originally published in Poem-a-Day on January 20, 2017, by the Academy of American Poets. Used by permission of the author.

"The Tree," by Jackleen Holton, was originally published in *Mobius: A Journal of Social Change*. Used by permission of the author.

"After the Fire," by Jodi Hottel, is from *Out of the Ashes*. Used by permission of the author.

Ron Koertge, "After Sun Yum Feng," from *Fever*, published by Red Hen Press. Used by permission of the author.

"Glass," by Danusha Lameris, originally appeared in the *Gettysburg Review*, and is forthcoming in *Bonfire Opera* as part of the Pitt Poetry Series. Used by permission of the author.

"It was 3 a.m., Winter, and Nine Miles from Truckee," by Suzanne Lummis, was originally published in *Plume* (plumepoetry.com). Used by permission of the author.

Kathleen McClung, "Gualala Winter" was published in the Maria W. Faust Sonnet Contest, in *LILIPOH*, and in *Fire & Rain: Ecopoetry of California*. Used by permission of the author.

"It's Only Dawn," by Penelope Moffat, was originally published in *Verse-Virtual*. Used by permission of the author.

"Ponderosa" by Claudia Monpere, was originally published in *Canary, A Literary Journal of the Environmental Crisis*. Used by permission of the author.

"Haiku Sonnet for San Francisco Climate," by Amanda Moore, was originally published in *Harbor Review*. Used by permission of the author.

Walter Pavlich, "Hardhat Pillow," from *Sensational Nightingales: Collected Poems of Walter Pavlich*, Lynx House Press, 2017, is used by permission of his executor Sandra McPherson.

Cindy Rinne, "Trees Have a Life Span — Jellyfish Live Forever" was first published by *Gap Toothed Madness* and appears in *Speaking Through Sediment*, co-authored with Michael Cooper. Used by permission of the author.

Maria Rosales, "Things I Discovered After," previously published in *Sisyphus* and *After/Ashes, a Camp Fire Anthology* by Butte College. Used by permission of the author.

Kim Scheiblauer, "Communion" was originally published in *phren-Z* under the title "Santa Rosa 2017." Used by permission of the author.

"An Offering" by SA Smythe, appeared in *We Have Never Asked Permission to Sing: Poetry Celebrating Trans Resilience*, commissioned poem-arts collabollation for Trans Day of Resilience Project 2019, Forward Together chapbook. Used by permission of the author.

"Control Burn," is copyright 1999 by Gary Snyder, from *The Gary Snyder Reader*. Reprinted by permission of Counterpoint Press.

Alison Turner, "No One Said It Would Be Easy," appeared in *What to Do in an Emergency*. Used by permission of the author.

"And because they slept in, my friends —" by Lenore Wilson was originally published in *Taos Review*. Used by permission of the author.

"Eye to eye, they solemnly convene to make the scene," from *Invisible Gifts* by Maw Shein Win. Copyright 2018 by Maw Shein Win. Used by permission of publisher Manic D Press.

[Untitled], by Gary Young originally appeared in *That's What I Thought*, Persea Books. Used by permission of the author and Persea Books.

APPRECIATIONS

Without the imagination and generosity of the Academy of American Poets, funded by the Mellon Foundation, you wouldn't be reading this anthology. To encourage poets working in civic positions in their communities, they dreamed up the Poets Laureate Fellowship that sparked this project. My deep thanks for the financial support for California Fire & Water, as well as for my own writing. I'm honored and happy to work beside the 12 other Poets Laureate in this inaugural year.

I'm grateful to the people who talked me into becoming Nevada County's first Poet Laureate, a job I did not want: Eliza Tudor, Nancy Shanteau, Sandy Frizzell, Indigo Moor, Judy Crowe, and Judie Rae. You were right, it was such a good idea and thanks for putting up with my surliness. Gratitude to Nevada County Arts Council and the Board of Supervisors of Nevada County for extending the invitation, and the residents of the county for engaging with poetry in so many ways.

Thanks to Jen Benka and friends, who added "counties" to the eligibility list. Thanks and love to all the poet-teachers and Meg Hamill at CalPoets, to my screeners and co-editors, Lisa Alvarez, Kirsten Casey, Chris Olander, and Julie Valin, and to the poets who organized anthology readings around the state (as of this writing), including Lea Aschkenas, Judy Bebelaar, Stella Beratlis, Maya Khosla, Danusha Lameris, Claudia Monpere, Sarah Pape, Connie Post, and Napa Bookmine. Thanks to Maxima Kahn and Julie Valin for their design chops, and to Lightning Source for helping me make small-batch, free-range, certified organic books so quickly.

I'm waving to my patrons on Patreon, who keep me sane and writing, and send out special gratitude to CALFIRE, Yubanet, and KVMR for the work they do locally to keep us from going up in smoke.

About the Academy of American Poets

The Academy of American Poets is the largest membership-based nonprofit organization fostering an appreciation for contemporary poetry and supporting American poets. The organization produces Poets.org, the world's largest publicly funded website for poets and poetry; originated and organizes National Poetry Month; publishes the popular Poem-a-Day series and American Poets magazine; creates and distributes Teach This Poem and other award-winning resources for K-12 educators; hosts an annual series of poetry readings and special events; and awards the American Poets Prizes. In addition, the Academy of American Poets coordinates a national Poetry Coalition working together to promote the value poets bring to our culture and the important contribution poetry makes in the lives of people of all ages and backgrounds. Executive Director: Jennifer Benka poets.org

About California Poets In the Schools

California Poets in the Schools empowers students of all ages throughout California to express their creativity, imagination, and intellectual curiosity through writing, performing and publishing their own poetry. We train and coordinate a multicultural network of published poets, who bring their passion and craft to public and private schools, juvenile halls, hospitals, libraries, and other community settings. Executive Director: Meg Hamill californiapoets.org

Many thanks to the Poet-Teachers who taught for this project: Tama Brisbane (Stanislaus/San Joaquin Counties), Kirsten Casey (Nevada County), Amanda Chiado (Hollister County), Brennan DeFrisco (Contra Costa County), Terri Glass (Marin County), Caroline Goodwin (San Mateo County), Catherine Hodges (Tulare County), Maureen Hurley (Alameda County), Christine Kravetz (Santa Barbara County), Michelle Krueger (Lake County), Daniel Zev Levinson (Humboldt/Trinity/Del Norte Counties), Seretta Martin (San Diego County), Blake More (Mendocino County), Johnnierennee Nelson (San Diego County), Chris Olander (Nevada County), Margo Perin (Sonoma County), Claudia Poquoc (San Diego County), Eva Poole-Gilson (Inyo/Mono Counties), Michele Rivers (Marin County), Fernando Albert Salinas (Ventura County), Kendra Tanacea (Sonoma County), Susie Terence (San Francisco County), Dawn Trook (Merced County), Jessica Wilson (Los Angeles County).